CHILDREN'S ENCYCLOPEDIA
SCIENCE

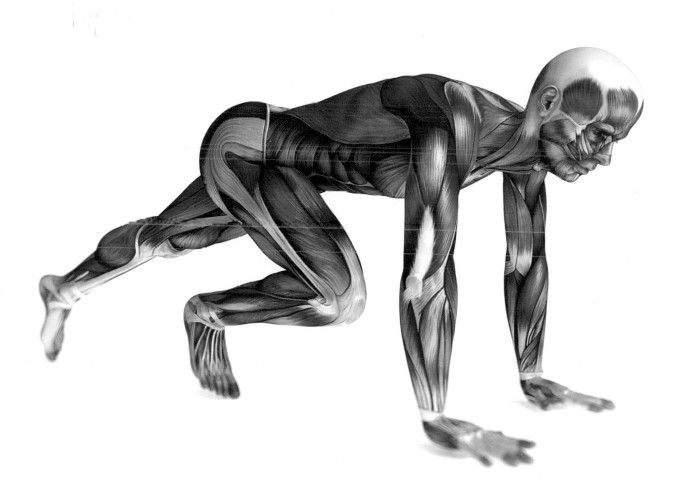

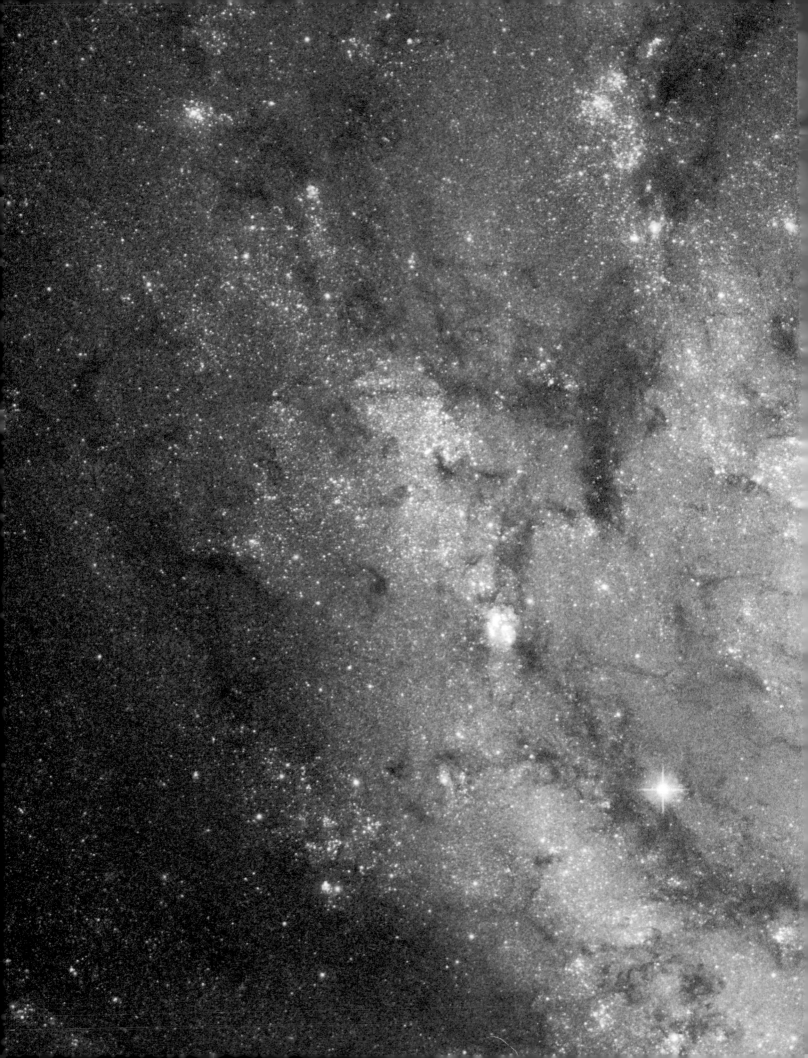

CHILDREN'S ENCYCLOPEDIA
SCIENCE

Miles
KeLLY

First published in 2013 by Miles Kelly Publishing Ltd
Harding's Barn, Bardfield End Green, Thaxted, Essex, CM6 3PX, UK

Copyright © Miles Kelly Publishing Ltd 2013

This edition printed 2015

4 6 8 10 9 7 5 3

Publishing Director Belinda Gallagher
Creative Director Jo Cowan
Editorial Director Rosie Neave
Cover Designer Simon Lee
Designers Jo Cowan, Kayleigh Allen, Rob Hale
Assistant Editor Amy Johnson
Indexer Gill Lee
Image Manager Liberty Newton
Production Elizabeth Collins, Caroline Kelly
Reprographics Stephan Davis, Thom Allaway, Jennifer Cozens
Contributors Sue Becklake, Duncan Brewer,
Clare Oliver, Steve Parker
Assets Lorraine King

ISBN 978-1-78209-111-0

Printed in China

British Library Cataloguing-in-Publication Data
A catalogue record for this book is available from the British Library

Made with paper from a sustainable forest

www.mileskelly.net
info@mileskelly.net

CONTENTS

SCIENCE 8–49

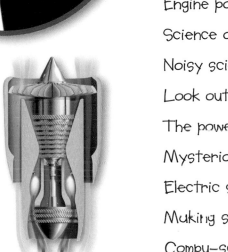

SPACE 50–91

WEATHER

92–133

HUMAN BODY

134–175

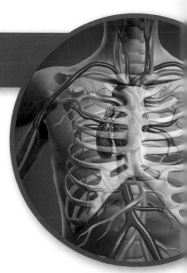

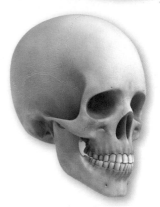

INVENTIONS

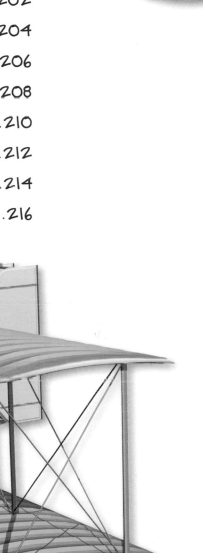

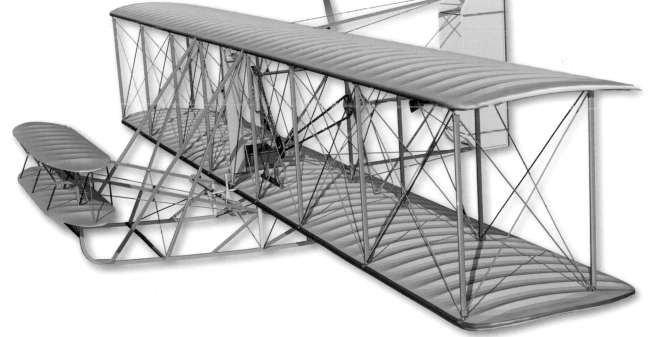

SCIENCE

1 Even one hundred books like this could not explain all the reasons why we need science. Toasters, bicycles, mobile phones, computers, cars, light bulbs – all the gadgets and machines we use every day are the results of scientific discoveries. Houses, skyscrapers, bridges and rockets are built using science. Our knowledge of medicines, nature, light and sound comes from science. Then there is the science of predicting the weather, investigating how stars shine, finding out why carrots are orange…

▼ In a big city, science is all around you – everything from sky-scraping buildings to speedy vehicles and useful gadgets is based on science and technology.

Machines big and small

2 **Machines are everywhere!** They help us do things, or make doing them easier. Every time you play on a see-saw, you are using a machine! A lever is a stiff bar that tilts at a point called the pivot or fulcrum. The pivot of the see-saw is in the middle. Using the see-saw as a lever, a small person can lift a big person by sitting further from the pivot.

▶ On a see-saw lever, the pivot is in the middle. Other levers have pivots at the end.

Thread

▶ Turning a screw moves it along with more force than the effort used to turn it.

3 **The screw is another simple but useful scientific machine.** It is a ridge, or thread, wrapped around a bar or pole. It changes a small turning motion into a powerful pulling or lifting movement. Wood screws hold together furniture or shelves. A car jack lets you lift up a whole car.

4 **Where would you be without wheels?** Not going very far. The wheel is a simple machine, a circular disc that turns around its centre on a bar called an axle. Wheels carry heavy weights easily. There are giant wheels on big trucks and trains and small wheels on rollerblades.

Axle

▼ Wheels reduce friction, allowing heavy loads to be carried more easily.

▼ Two pulleys together reduce the force needed to lift a heavy girder by one half.

5 A pulley turns around, like a wheel. It has a groove around its edge for a cable or rope. Lots of pulleys allow us to lift very heavy weights easily. The pulleys on a tower crane can lift huge steel girders to the top of a skyscraper.

▲ Bicycle gears let you pedal at the same speed, with the same force, when climbing up a hill or speeding down it.

Reversing gears

Sliding rack

Pinion gear

Bevel gears

Slow pinion gear

Screw-shaped worm gear

▲ Gears change the turning direction of a force. They can slow it down or speed it up — and even convert it into a sliding force (rack and pinion).

Pivot

Lever

I DON'T BELIEVE IT!

A ramp is a simple machine called an inclined plane. It is easier to walk up a ramp than to jump straight to the top.

6 Gears are like wheels, with pointed teeth around the edges. They change a fast, weak turning force into a slow, powerful one – or the other way around. On a bike, you can pedal up the steepest hill in bottom gear, then speed down the other side in top gear.

When science is hot!

7 The science of heat is important in lots of ways. Not only do we cook with heat, but we also use it to warm our homes and heat water. Burning takes place inside the engines of cars, trucks, planes and rockets. It is also used in factory processes, from making steel to shaping plastics.

▲ A firework burns suddenly as an explosive, producing heat, light and sound. The 'bang' is the sound made by the paper wrapper as it is blown apart.

Heat from the drink is conducted up the metal spoon

8 **Heat can move by conduction.** A hot object will pass on, or transfer, some of its heat to a cooler one. Dip a metal spoon in a hot drink and the spoon handle soon warms up. Heat is conducted from the drink, through the metal.

9 **Heat moves by invisible 'heat rays'.** This is called thermal radiation and the rays are infrared waves. Our planet is warmed by the Sun because heat from the Sun radiates through space as infrared waves.

TRUE OR FALSE?

1. Burning happens inside the engine of a plane.
2. A device for measuring temperature is called a calendar.
3. Heat rays are known as infrablue waves.

Answers:
1. True 2. False 3. False

◀ Metal is a good conductor of heat. Put a teaspoon in a hot drink and feel how quickly it heats up.

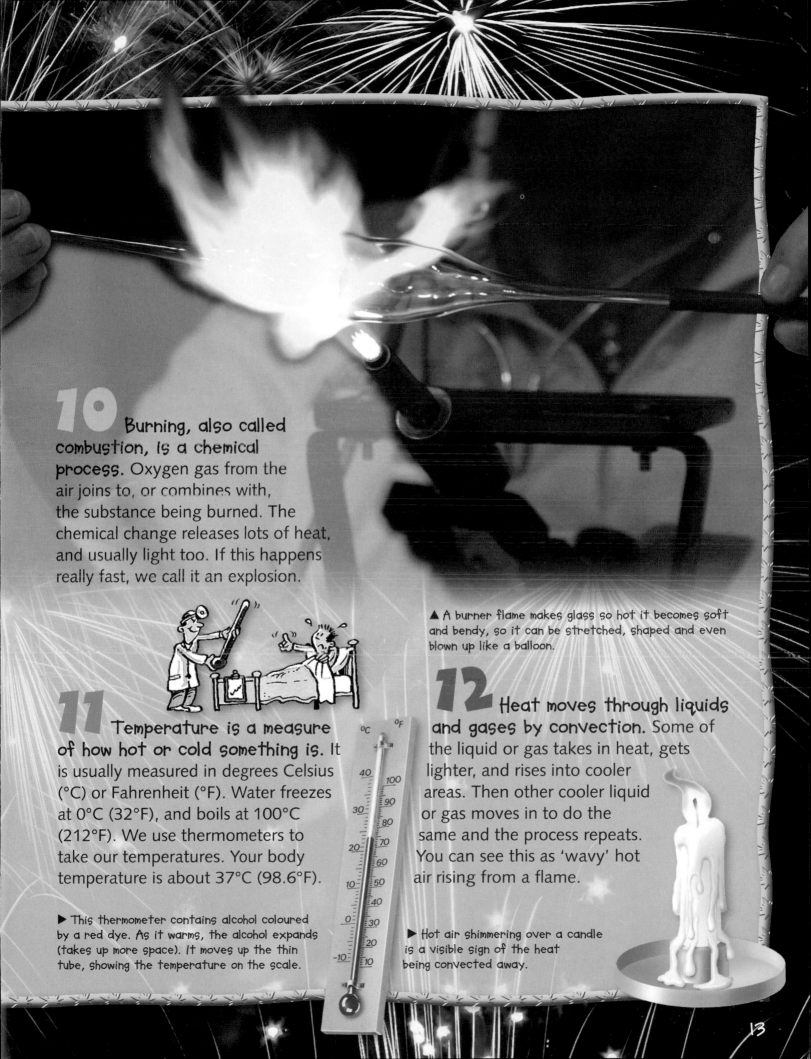

10 Burning, also called combustion, is a chemical process. Oxygen gas from the air joins to, or combines with, the substance being burned. The chemical change releases lots of heat, and usually light too. If this happens really fast, we call it an explosion.

▲ A burner flame makes glass so hot it becomes soft and bendy, so it can be stretched, shaped and even blown up like a balloon.

11 Temperature is a measure of how hot or cold something is. It is usually measured in degrees Celsius (°C) or Fahrenheit (°F). Water freezes at 0°C (32°F), and boils at 100°C (212°F). We use thermometers to take our temperatures. Your body temperature is about 37°C (98.6°F).

▶ This thermometer contains alcohol coloured by a red dye. As it warms, the alcohol expands (takes up more space). It moves up the thin tube, showing the temperature on the scale.

12 Heat moves through liquids and gases by convection. Some of the liquid or gas takes in heat, gets lighter, and rises into cooler areas. Then other cooler liquid or gas moves in to do the same and the process repeats. You can see this as 'wavy' hot air rising from a flame.

▶ Hot air shimmering over a candle is a visible sign of the heat being convected away.

Engine power

13 Imagine having to walk or run everywhere, instead of riding in a car. Engines are machines that use fuel to do work for us and make life easier. Fuel is a substance that has chemical energy stored inside it. The energy is released as heat by burning or exploding the fuel in the engine.

▼ A jet engine has sets of angled blades, called turbines, that spin on shafts.

Turbines squash incoming air

Jet fuel is sprayed into the air inside the chamber, creating a small explosion

Burning gases spin exhaust turbines

14 Most cars have petrol engines. An air and petrol mixture is pushed into a hollow chamber called a cylinder. A spark from a spark plug makes it explode, which pushes a piston down inside the cylinder. This movement is used by gears to turn the wheels. Most cars have four or six cylinders.

15 A diesel engine doesn't use sparks. The mixture of air and diesel is squashed in the cylinder, becoming so hot it explodes. Diesel engines are used in machines such as tractors that need lots of power.

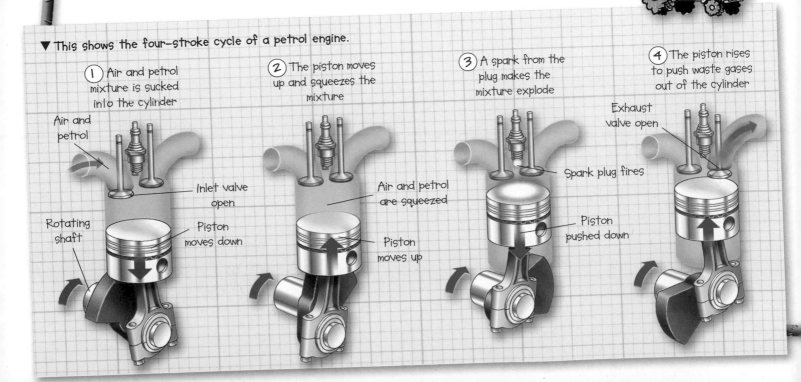

▼ This shows the four-stroke cycle of a petrol engine.

① Air and petrol mixture is sucked into the cylinder

② The piston moves up and squeezes the mixture

③ A spark from the plug makes the mixture explode

④ The piston rises to push waste gases out of the cylinder

Air and petrol

Rotating shaft

Inlet valve open

Piston moves down

Air and petrol are squeezed

Piston moves up

Spark plug fires

Piston pushed down

Exhaust valve open

▲ On a fast jet plane at full power, the exhaust gases from the engines glow almost white-hot.

16 A jet engine mixes air and kerosene and sets fire to it in one long, continuous, roaring explosion. Incredibly hot gases blast out of the back of the engine. These push the engine forward – along with the plane.

17 An electric motor passes electricity through coils of wire. This makes the coils magnetic, and they push or pull against magnets around them. The push-pull makes the coils spin on their shaft (axle).

▼ Using magnetic forces, an electric motor turns electrical energy into moving or kinetic energy.

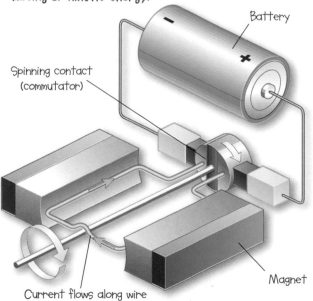

Battery

Spinning contact (commutator)

Current flows along wire

Magnet

18 Engines that burn fuel give out gases and particles through their exhausts. Some of these gases are harmful to the environment. The less we use engines, the better. Electric motors are quiet, efficient and reliable, but they still need fuel – to make the electricity at the power station.

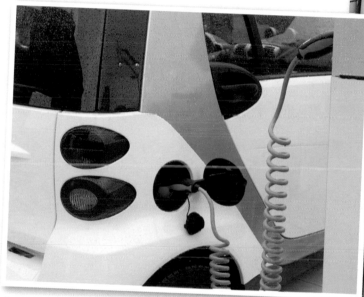

▲ Electric cars have sets of batteries to turn the motor. The batteries are 'filled' with electrical energy by plugging into a recharging point.

QUIZ

1. Are exhaust gases good for the environment?
2. Does a diesel engine use sparks?
3. How many cylinders do most cars have?
4. Do electric cars have batteries?

Answers:
1. No, some of them are harmful 2. No 3. Four or six 4. Yes

Science on the move

19 Without science, you would have to walk everywhere, or ride a horse. Luckily, scientists and engineers have developed many methods of transport, most importantly, the car. Lots of people can travel together in a bus, train, plane or ship. These use less energy and resources, and make less pollution than cars.

▼ Modern airports are enormous. They can stretch for several miles, and they have a constant flow of planes taking off and landing. Hundreds of people are needed to make sure that everything runs smoothly and on time.

Passenger terminal

Jetway

20 Science is used to stop criminals. Science-based security measures include a 'door frame' that detects metal objects like guns and a scanner that sees inside bags. A sniffer-machine can detect the smell of explosives or illegal drugs.

QUIZ

1. How do air traffic controllers talk to pilots?
2. What does a red train signal mean?
3. What powers the supports that move jetways?

Answers:
1. By radio 2. Stop 3. Electric motors

21 Jetways are extending walkways that stretch out from the passenger terminal right to the planes' doors. Their supports move along on wheeled trolleys driven by electric motors.

22 Every method of transport needs to be safe and on time. In the airport control tower, air traffic controllers track planes on radar screens. They talk to pilots by radio. Beacons send out radio signals, giving the direction and distance to the airport.

▶ The radar screen shows each aircraft as a blip, with its flight number or identity code.

IB-57
Q-74
CP-35
UA-154
L-47
AA-127
EJ-244
BA-76
BY-47
BA-277
RA-147
10 20 30 40 50 60
Q-35
CP-87
KL-163
AA-45
JAL-372
KL-89
L-178

23 On the road, drivers obey traffic lights. On a railway network, train drivers obey similar signal lights of different colours, such as red for stop. Sensors by the track record each train passing and send the information by wires or radio to the control room. Each train's position is shown as a flashing light on a wall map.

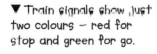

▼ Train signals show just two colours – red for stop and green for go.

D-27

▶ Trackside switches and detectors react to a train going past and automatically change the signals, so that a following train does not get too close.

02

Noisy science

Listening to the radio or television, playing music, shouting at each other — they all depend on the science of sound — acoustics. Sounds are carried by invisible waves in the air. The waves are areas of low pressure, where air particles are stretched farther apart, alternating with areas of high pressure, where they are squashed closer together.

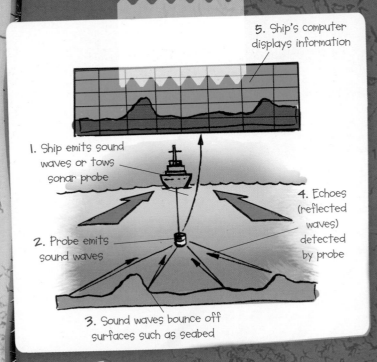

5. Ship's computer displays information

1. Ship emits sound waves or tows sonar probe

2. Probe emits sound waves

3. Sound waves bounce off surfaces such as seabed

4. Echoes (reflected waves) detected by probe

25 Scientists measure the loudness or intensity of sound in decibels, dB. A very quiet sound like a ticking watch is 10 dB. Ordinary speech is 50–60 dB. Loud music is 90 dB. A jet plane taking off is 120 dB. Too much noise damages the ears.

◄ In sonar (echo-sounding), sound waves in the water bounce or reflect off objects, and are detected.

Atomic explosion

Jet plane

26 Whether a sound is high or low is called its pitch, or frequency. It is measured in Hertz, Hz. A singing bird or whining motorcycle has a high pitch. A rumble of thunder or a massive truck has a low pitch. People can hear frequencies from 25 to 20,000 Hz.

Express train

Whisper

▶ The decibel scale measures the intensity, or energy, in sound.

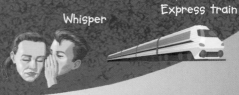

| 0 dB | 40 dB | 80 dB | 120 dB | 180 dB |

27

Sound waves spread out from a vibrating object that is moving rapidly to and fro. Stretch an elastic band between your fingers and twang it. As it vibrates, it makes a sound. When you speak, vocal cords in your neck vibrate. You can feel them through your skin.

28

Sound waves travel about 330 metres every second. This is fast, but it is one million times slower than light waves. Sound waves also bounce off hard, flat surfaces. This is called reflection. The returning waves are heard as an echo.

29

Loudspeakers change electrical signals into sounds. The signals in the wire pass through a wire coil inside the speaker. This turns the coil into a magnet, which pushes and pulls against another magnet. The pushing and pulling make the cone vibrate, which sends sound waves into the air.

◄ The word 'sonic' means making sounds, and the high-pitched noises of bats can be described as 'ultrasonic' – too high for us to hear.

Echoes bouncing back off the moth

Sound waves from the bat

▲ Bats make high-pitched sounds. If the sounds hit an insect they bounce back to the bat's ears. The reflected sound (echo) gives the bat information about the size and location of the insect.

BOX GUITAR

You will need:

shoebox   elastic band
split pins   card

Cut a hole about 10 centimetres across on one side of an empty shoebox. Push split pins through either side of the hole, and stretch an elastic band between them. Pluck the band. Hear how the air and box vibrate. Cover the hole with card. Is the 'guitar' as loud?

Look out – light's about!

30 Almost everything you do depends on light and the science of light, which is called optics. Light is a form of energy that you can see. Light waves are made of electricity and magnetism – and they are tiny. About 2000 of them laid end to end would stretch across this full stop.

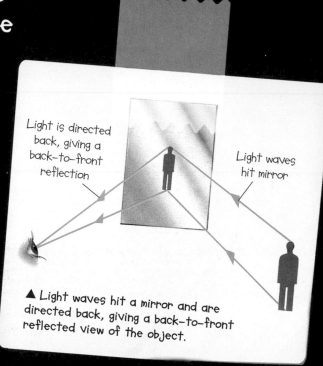

Light is directed back, giving a back-to-front reflection

Light waves hit mirror

▲ Light waves hit a mirror and are directed back, giving a back-to-front reflected view of the object.

▲ A prism of clear glass or clear plastic separates the colours in white light.

32 Like sound, light bounces off surfaces that are very smooth. This is called reflection. A mirror is smooth, hard and flat. When you look at it, you see your reflection.

31 Ordinary light from the Sun or from a light bulb is called white light. But when white light passes through a prism, a triangular block of clear glass, it splits into many colours. These colours are known as the spectrum. Each colour has a different length of wave. A rainbow is made by raindrops, which work like millions of tiny prisms to split up sunlight.

33 Light passes through certain materials, like clear glass and plastic. Materials that let light pass through, to give a clear view, are transparent. Those that do not allow light through, like wood and metal, are opaque.

34 Mirrors and lenses are important parts of many optical (light–using) gadgets. They are found in cameras, binoculars, microscopes, telescopes and lasers. Without them, we would have no close-up photographs of tiny microchips or insects or giant planets   in fact, no photos at all.

I DON'T BELIEVE IT!
Light is the fastest thing in the Universe – it travels through space at 300,000 kilometres per second. That's seven times around the world in less than one second!

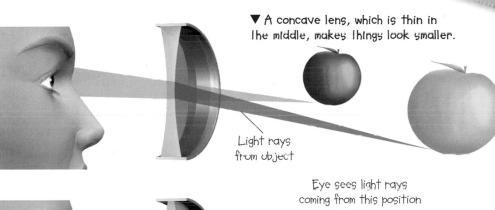

▼ A concave lens, which is thin in the middle, makes things look smaller.

Light rays from object

Eye sees light rays coming from this position

▲ A convex lens, which bulges in the middle, makes things look larger.

35 Light does not usually go straight through glass. It bends slightly where it goes into the glass, then bends back as it comes out. This is called refraction. A lens is a curved piece of glass or plastic that bends light to make things look bigger, smaller or clearer. Spectacle and contact lenses bend light to help people see more clearly.

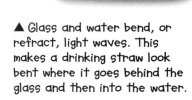

▲ Glass and water bend, or refract, light waves. This makes a drinking straw look bent where it goes behind the glass and then into the water.

36 Laser light is a special kind of light. Like ordinary light, it is made of waves, but it has three main differences. Ordinary white light is a mixture of colours, while laser light is one pure colour. Ordinary light waves have peaks (highs) and troughs (lows), which do not line up – laser light waves line up perfectly. Lastly, ordinary light spreads and fades. A laser beam can travel for thousands of kilometres as a strong, straight beam.

◄ The narrow horizontal beam from a laser spirit level can shine all the way across a building site.

▼ Waves of light build up and bounce to and fro inside a laser, then emerge at one end.

Silver mirror

Part-silver mirror

Particles in ruby crystal

Laser beam emerges

37 To make a laser beam, energy is fed in short bursts into a substance called the active medium. The energy might be electricity, heat or ordinary light. In a red ruby laser, the active medium is a rod of ruby crystal. A strong lamp makes the particles in the crystal vibrate. The energy they give off bounces to and fro inside the crystal. Eventually, the rays vibrate with each other and they are all the same length. The energy becomes so strong that it bursts through a mirror at one end of the crystal.

Beam bounces off CD

Laser

Spinning CD

Reflected beam passes through prism

Laser beam bent by prism

Reflected beam detected by sensor

▲ A CD laser detects tiny pits in the disc's underside.

▲ In a spectacular outdoor light show, different coloured laser beams sweep to and fro as they pierce the darkness, seemingly all the way into space.

38 Lasers were invented in 1960. They are used to play CDs and DVDs for music and movies, and in computers. They cut through thick metal in factories, and carry out delicate eye operations. They carry phone calls and television programmes along cables. They even measure movements of the Earth to warn of volcanoes or earthquakes.

QUIZ

1. How far can laser beams travel?
2. When were lasers invented?
3. Which everyday machines use lasers?

Answers:
1. Thousands of kilometres
2. 1960 3. DVD players, CD players, computers

◀ An industrial laser has the power to melt metal into gas and cut a neat line.

23

Mysterious magnets

39 Without magnets there would be no electric motors, computers or loudspeakers. Magnetism is an invisible force to do with atoms – tiny particles that make up everything. Atoms are made of even smaller particles, including electrons. Magnetism is linked to the way that these line up and move. Most magnetic substances contain iron. As iron makes up a big part of the metallic substance steel, steel is also magnetic.

▶ For metal recycling, an electromagnet lifts out only iron–containing or ferrous metals, such as steel.

40 A magnet is a lump of iron or steel that has all its electrons and atoms lined up. This means that their magnetic forces all add up. The force surrounds the magnet, in a region called the magnetic field. This is strongest at the two parts of the magnet called the poles.

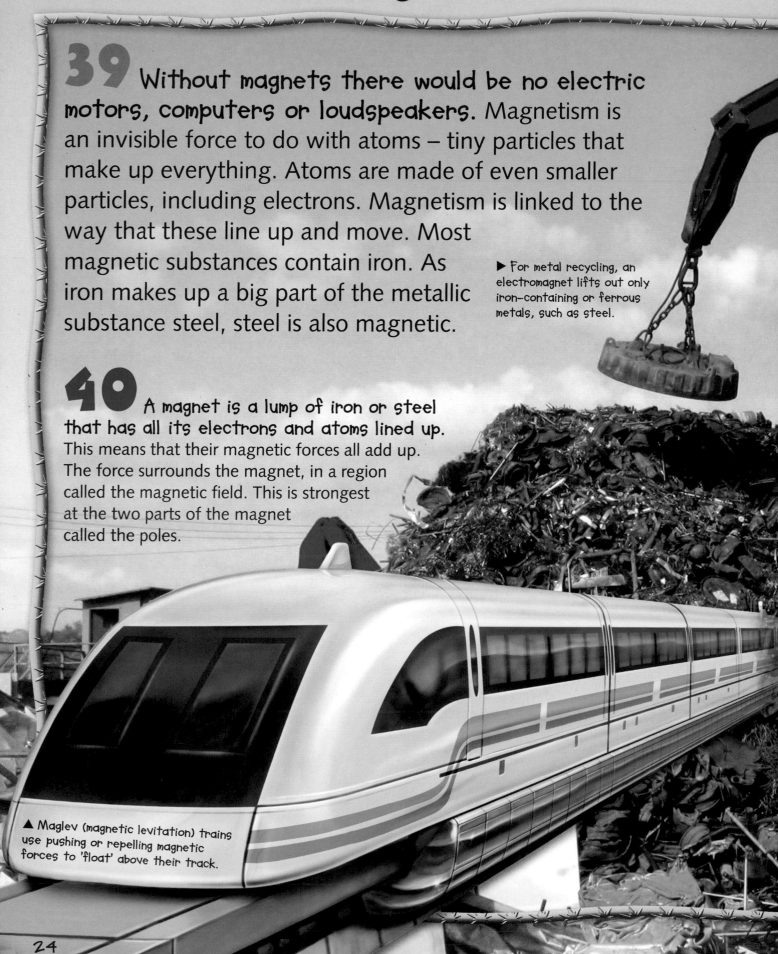

▲ Maglev (magnetic levitation) trains use pushing or repelling magnetic forces to 'float' above their track.

42 When electricity flows through a wire, it makes a weak magnetic field around it. If the wire is wrapped into a coil, the magnetism becomes stronger. This is called an electromagnet. Its magnetic force is the same as an ordinary magnet, but when the electricity goes off, the magnetism does too. Some electromagnets are so strong, they can lift whole cars.

A magnet has two different poles — north and south. A north pole repels (pushes away) the north pole of another magnet. Two south poles also repel each other. But a north pole and a south pole attract (pull together). Both magnetic poles attract any substance containing iron, like a nail or a screw.

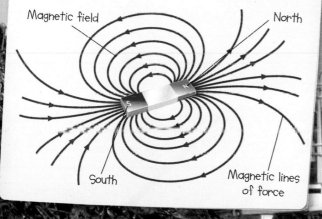

▼ The field around a magnet affects objects that contain iron.

Magnetic field

North

South

Magnetic lines of force

QUIZ

Which of these substances or objects is magnetic?

1. Steel spoon 2. Plastic spoon
3. Pencil 4. Drinks can
5. Food can 6. Screwdriver
7. Cooking foil

Answers:
1. Yes 2. No 3. No
4. No 5. Yes 6. Yes 7. No

Electric sparks!

43 Flick a switch and things happen. The television goes off, the computer comes on, lights shine and music plays. Electricity is our favourite form of energy. We send it along wires and plug hundreds of machines into it.

▼ When an electric current flows, the electrons (small blue balls) all move the same way, jumping from one atom to the next. (The red balls are the centres or nuclei of the atoms.)

44 Electricity depends on electrons. In certain substances, when electrons are 'pushed', they hop from one atom to the next. When billions do this every second, electricity flows. The 'push' is from a battery or a generator. Electricity only flows in a complete loop or circuit. Break the circuit, and the flow stops.

Atom

Electron

▼ Solar panels contain many hundreds of fingernail-sized PV (photovoltaic) cells. These convert light energy ('photo') to electrical energy ('voltaic').

▼ A battery has a chemical paste inside its metal casing.

Positive contact

Negative contact on base

45 A battery makes electricity from chemicals. Two different chemicals next to each other, such as an acid and a metal, swap electrons and get the flow going. Electricity's pushing strength is measured in volts. Most batteries are about 1.5, 3, 6 or 9 volts, with 12 volts in cars.

46 Electricity flows easily through some substances, including water and metals. These are electrical conductors. Other substances do not allow electricity to flow. They are insulators. Insulators include wood, plastic, glass, card and ceramics. Metal wires and cables have coverings of plastic, to stop the electricity leaking away.

47 Electricity from power stations is carried along cables on high pylons, or buried underground. This is known as the distribution grid. At thousands of volts, this electricity is extremely dangerous. For use in the home, it is changed to 220 volts (in the UK).

▼ Electricity generators are housed in huge casings, some bigger than trucks.

Pylon holds cables off the ground

◀ To check and repair high–voltage cables, the electricity must be turned off well in advance.

48 Mains electricity is made at a power station. A fuel such as coal or oil is burned to heat water into high-pressure steam. The steam pushes past the blades of a turbine and makes them spin. The turbines turn generators, which have wire coils near powerful magnets, and the spinning motion makes electricity flow in the coils.

MAKE A CIRCUIT
You will need:
lightbulb   battery   wire
plastic ruler   metal spoon   dry card
Join a bulb to a battery with pieces of wire, as shown. Electricity flows round the circuit and lights the bulb. Make a gap in the circuit and put various objects into it, to see if they allow electricity to flow again. Try a plastic ruler, a metal spoon and some dry card.

Making sounds and pictures

49 The air is full of waves we cannot see or hear, unless we have the right machine. Radio waves are a form of electrical and magnetic energy, just like heat and light waves, microwaves and X-rays. All of these are called electromagnetic waves and they travel at an equal speed – the speed of light.

Satellite

Radio waves

51 Radio waves carry their information by being altered, or modulated, in a certain pattern. The height of a wave is called its amplitude. If this is altered, it is known as AM (amplitude modulation). Look for AM on the radio display.

50 Radio waves are used for both radio and television. They travel vast distances. Long waves curve around the Earth's surface. Short waves bounce between the Earth and the sky.

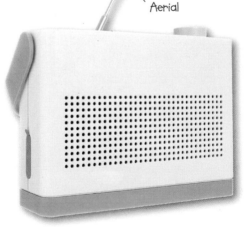

Aerial

52 The number of waves per second is called the frequency. If this is altered, it is known as FM (frequency modulation). FM radio is clearer than AM, and less affected by weather and thunderstorms.

▼ This range of waves, with different wavelengths, are electrical and magnetic energy. They are called the electromagnetic spectrum.

▲ A radio set picks up radio waves using its aerial or antenna.

Long radio waves	Shorter radio waves (TV)	Microwaves	Infrared waves	Light waves (visible light)	Ultraviolet rays	X-rays	Short X-rays	Gamma rays

53 Radio waves are sent out, or transmitted, from antennae on tall masts or on satellites, to reach a very wide area. A radio receiver converts the pattern of waves to sounds. A television receiver or TV set changes them to pictures and sounds.

▼ A dish-shaped receiver picks up radio waves for TV channels.

54 Digital radio uses incredibly short bursts of radio waves with gaps between them – many thousands each second. Each burst represents the digit (number) 1, and a gap is 0. The order of the 1s and 0s carries information in the form of binary code, as in a computer.

▶ A plasma screen has thousands of tiny boxes, or cells, of three colours – red, green and blue. Electric pulses heat the gas inside for a split second into plasma, which gives out a burst of light. Combinations of these colours gives all the other colours.

▼ Flat-screen TVs can be LCD or plasma. They use less electricity than cathode-ray TVs and produce a better picture.

KEY
1. Glowing 'on' cell
2. Dark 'off' cell
3. Rear grid of electrical contacts
4. – 6. Coloured phosphors inside cells
7. Backing plate
8. Front grid of electrical contacts
9. Transparent front cover

Compu-science

55 Computers are amazing machines, but they have to be told exactly what to do. So we put in instructions and information, by various means. These include typing on a keyboard, inserting a disc or memory stick, downloading from the Internet, using a joystick or games controller, or linking up a camera, scanner or another computer.

56 Most computers are controlled by instructions from a keyboard and a mouse. The mouse moves a pointer around on the screen and its click buttons select choices from lists called menus.

Flat screen monitor

USB (Universal Serial Bus) sockets

External monitor (screen) socket

Headphone socket

Silicon 'wafer'

Plastic casing

Wire 'feet' link to other part in the computer

◄ This close up of a slice of silicon 'wafer' shows the tiny parts that receive and send information in a computer.

57 Some computers are controlled by talking to them! They pick up the sounds using a microphone. This is speech recognition technology.

58 The 'main brain' of a computer is its Central Processing Unit. It is usually a microchip – millions of electronic parts on a chip of silicon, hardly larger than a fingernail. It receives information and instructions from other microchips, carries out the work, and sends back the results.

QUIZ

You may have heard of these sets of letters. Do you know what they mean? Their full written-out versions are all here on these two pages.
1. RAM 2. ROM
3. CPU

Answers:
1. Random Access Memory
2. Read Only Memory
3. Central Processing Unit

▲ Launched in 2010, the Apple iPad began a new trend in computerized devices called 'tablets'.

▼ The keys on a keyboard have bendy metal contacts that come together when pressed, allowing electricity to flow.

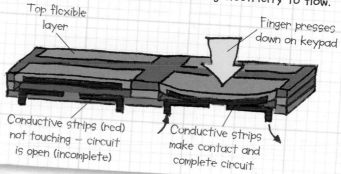

Top flexible layer

Finger presses down on keypad

Conductive strips (red) not touching – circuit is open (incomplete)

Conductive strips make contact and complete circuit

CD or DVD drive reader

Mouse pad

Keyboard

▲ As well as desktop computers, there are also laptops with a fold-up LCD (liquid crystal display) screen. Touching the mouse pad with a finger controls the cursor or insert point on the screen.

59 Information and instructions are contained in the computer in memory microchips. There are two kinds. Random Access Memory is like a jotting pad. It keeps changing as the computer carries out its tasks. Read Only Memory is like an instruction book. It usually contains the instructions for how the computer starts up and how all the microchips work together.

60 A computer usually displays its progress on a monitor screen. It feeds information to output devices such as printers, loudspeakers and robot arms. Information can be stored on CDs, DVDs, memory sticks (chips), external HDs (hard drive discs), or uploaded to the Internet.

Web around the world

61 The world is at your fingertips — if you are on the Internet. The Internet is one of the most amazing results of science. It is a worldwide network of computers, linked like one huge electrical spider's web.

62 Signals travel between computers in many ways. These include electricity along telephone wires, flashes of laser light along fibre-optic cables or radio waves between tall towers. Information is changed from one form to another in a split second. It can also travel between computers on different sides of the world in less than a second using satellite links.

First 'private' Internet, ARPANET, for the US military

Joint Academic Network (JANET) connects UK universities via their own Internet

Yahoo! Launches as a 'Guide to the World Wide Web' — what we now call a browser or search engine

Animation starts to become common on websites

1969   **1984**   **1994**   **1996**

1961   **1972**   **1989**   **1995**

First ideas for 'packet switching', the basic way the Internet parcels up and sends information in small blocks or packets

First emails, mostly on ARPANET

The birth of the Internet as we know it today, when Tim Berners-Lee and the team at CERN invent the World Wide Web to make information easier to publish and access

eBay and Amazon booksellers begin, and online trade starts to rise

63 The World Wide Web is public information that anyone can find on the Internet, available for everyone to see. However, sometimes you have to pay or join a club to get to certain parts of it. A website is a collection of related information, usually made up of text, videos and pictures. There might be hundreds of web pages within each website. Email is the system for sending private messages from one person to another.

I DON'T BELIEVE IT!

The World Wide Web is the best known and most widely used part of the Internet system. It has billions of pages of information.

▼ Many mobile phones can be used to access the Internet, allowing users to browse web pages, send emails and watch videos.

Facebook has fewer new users signing up — is the slower growth temporary, or the beginning of the end for online social networking?

Half of households in the UK have Internet connections

YouTube is launched, allowing video sharing

The first iPhones bring mobile Internet use for almost anyone

2003   2005   2007   2011

1998   2004   2006   2010

Google is launched as a rival to Yahoo!

Facebook is launched, starting the trend for social networking over the Internet

Twitter is launched for posting and sharing text messages, but has a slow start

HD (High Definition) Internet video links become more practical

▲ The Web and the Internet interact with other technologies. Twitter is an online public version of text-only messages called 'tweets' developed from mobile phone 'texting' (SMS, Short Message Service).

What's it made of?

64 You wouldn't make a bridge out of straw, or a cup out of bubblewrap! Choosing the right substance for the job is important. All the substances in the world can be divided into several groups. For example, metals such as iron, silver and gold are strong, hard and shiny, and conduct heat and electricity well. They are used to make things that have to be strong and long-lasting.

65 Plastics are made mainly from the substances in petroleum (crude oil). There are so many kinds — some are hard and brittle while others are soft and bendy. They are usually long-lasting, not affected by weather or damp, and they resist heat and electricity.

KEY

① The front wing is a special shape — this produces a force that presses the car down onto the track

② The main body of the car is made from carbon fibre, a light but very strong material

③ The car's axles are made from titanium — a very strong, light metal

④ The engine is made from various alloys, or mixtures of metals, based on aluminium. It produces up to ten times the power of a family car engine

⑤ Each tyre is made of thick, tough rubber to withstand high speeds

⑥ The rear wing is also carbon fibre composite

▼ A racing car has thousands of parts made from hundreds of materials. Each is suited to certain conditions such as stress, temperature and vibrations.

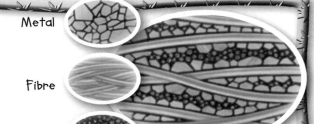

Metal

Fibre

Ceramic

▲ Metal, fibre and ceramic can combine to make a composite material. The way all of these ingredients are arranged can affect the composite's strength.

◀ In 2007, the Interstate 35W bridge collapsed in Minneapolis, USA, killing 13 people. It was due to cracking of small steel connecting plates that were too thin for the weight.

66 Ceramics are materials based on clay or other substances dug from the Earth. They can be shaped and dried, like a clay bowl. Or they can be fired – baked in a hot oven called a kiln. This makes them hard and long-lasting, but brittle and prone to cracks. Ceramics resist heat and electricity very well.

67 Glass is produced from the raw substances limestone and sand. When heated at a high temperature, these substances become a clear, gooey liquid, which sets hard as it cools. Its great advantage is that you can see through it.

68 Composites are mixtures or combinations of different materials. For example, glass strands are coated with plastic to make GRP – glass-reinforced plastic. This composite has the advantages of both materials.

MAKE YOUR OWN COMPOSITE

You will need:

flour   newspaper strips
water   balloon   pin

You can make a composite called pâpier maché from flour, newspaper and water. Tear newspaper into strips. Mix flour and water into a paste. Dip each strip in the paste and place it around a blown-up balloon. Cover the balloon and allow it to dry. Pop the balloon with a pin, and the composite should stay in shape.

World of chemicals

69 The world is made of chemical substances. Some are completely pure. Others are mixtures of substances – such as petroleum (crude oil). Petroleum provides us with thousands of different chemicals and materials, such as plastics, paints, soaps and fuels. It is one of the most useful, and valuable, substances in the world.

The fumes cool as they rise up the tower, causing them to condense

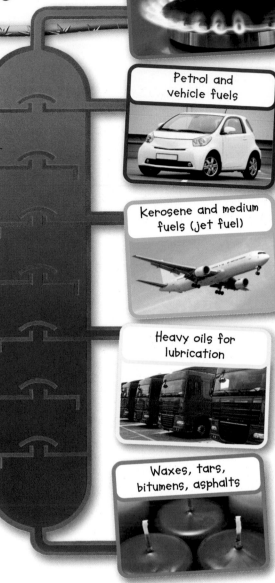

Fuel gases for burning

Petrol and vehicle fuels

Kerosene and medium fuels (jet fuel)

Heavy oils for lubrication

Waxes, tars, bitumens, asphalts

Furnace

Crude oil is super-heated and some parts turn into fumes

▼ The biggest offshore oil platforms are more than 150 metres tall above the ocean surface. They drill boreholes into the seabed and pump up the crude oil, or petroleum.

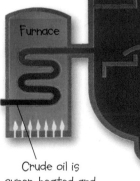

▲ The huge tower (fractionating column) of an oil refinery may be 100 metres high.

70 In an oil refinery, crude oil is heated in a huge tower. Some of its different substances turn into fumes and rise up the tower. The fumes condense (turn back into liquids) at different heights inside, due to the different temperatures at each level. Thick, gooey tars, asphalts and bitumens – used to make road surfaces – remain at the bottom.

71

One group of chemicals is called acids. They vary in strength from very weak citric acid, which gives the sharp taste to fruits such as lemons, to extremely strong and dangerous sulphuric acid in a car battery. Powerful acids burn and corrode, or eat away, substances. Some even corrode glass or steel.

72

Another group of chemicals is bases. They vary in strength from weak alkaloids, which give the bitter taste to coffee beans, to strong and dangerous bases in drain cleaners and industrial polishes. Bases feel soapy or slimy and, like acids, they can burn or corrode.

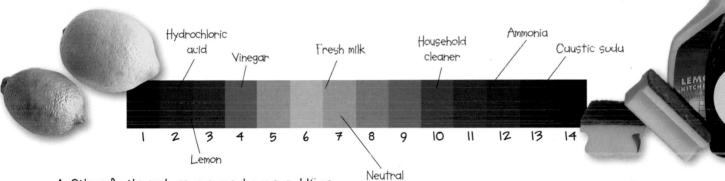

Hydrochloric acid
Vinegar
Fresh milk
Household cleaner
Ammonia
Caustic soda

1　2　3　4　5　6　7　8　9　10　11　12　13　14

Lemon
Neutral

▲ Citrus fruits such as oranges, lemons and limes have a tart taste because they contain a mild acid, called citric acid. It has a pH of 3.

▲ Household cleaners often contain alkalis to help them break down grease and fat. Some cleaners have a pH of 10.

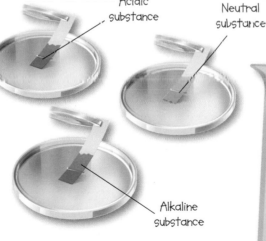

Acidic substance
Neutral substance

▶ Indicator paper changes colour when it touches different substances. Acids turn it red, alkalis make it bluish–purple. The deeper the colour, the stronger the acid or base.

Alkaline substance

73

Acids and bases are 'opposite' types of chemicals. When they meet, they undergo changes called a chemical reaction. The result is usually a third type of chemical, called a salt. The common salt we use for cooking is one example. Its chemical name is sodium chloride.

FROTHY FUN

You will need:
vinegar　washing soda

Create a chemical reaction by adding a few drops of vinegar to a spoonful of washing soda in a saucer. The vinegar is an acid, the soda is a base. The two react by frothing and giving off bubbles of carbon dioxide gas. What is left is a salt (but not to be eaten).

74 The world seems to be made of millions of different substances – such as soil, wood, concrete, plastics and air. These are combinations of simpler substances. If you could take them apart, you would see that they are made of pure substances called elements.

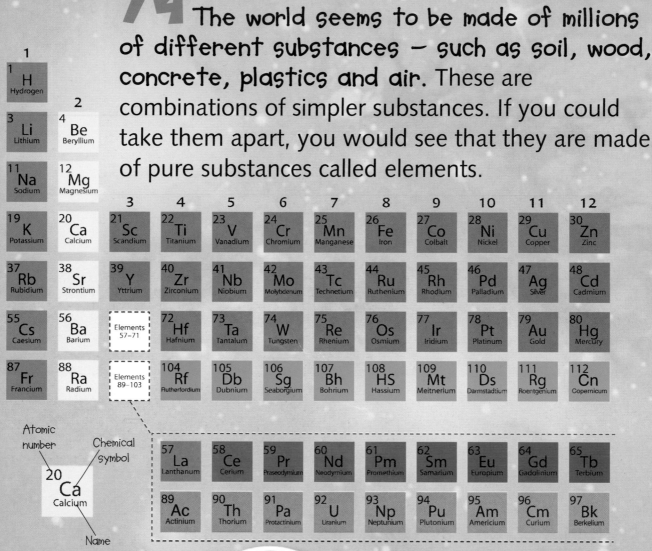

1											
1 **H** Hydrogen	2										
3 **Li** Lithium	4 **Be** Beryllium										
11 **Na** Sodium	12 **Mg** Magnesium	3	4	5	6	7	8	9	10	11	12
19 **K** Potassium	20 **Ca** Calcium	21 **Sc** Scandium	22 **Ti** Titanium	23 **V** Vanadium	24 **Cr** Chromium	25 **Mn** Manganese	26 **Fe** Iron	27 **Co** Colbalt	28 **Ni** Nickel	29 **Cu** Copper	30 **Zn** Zinc
37 **Rb** Rubidium	38 **Sr** Strontium	39 **Y** Yttrium	40 **Zr** Zirconium	41 **Nb** Niobium	42 **Mo** Molybdenum	43 **Tc** Technetium	44 **Ru** Ruthenium	45 **Rh** Rhodium	46 **Pd** Palladium	47 **Ag** Silver	48 **Cd** Cadmium
55 **Cs** Caesium	56 **Ba** Barium	Elements 57–71	72 **Hf** Hafnium	73 **Ta** Tantalum	74 **W** Tungsten	75 **Re** Rhenium	76 **Os** Osmium	77 **Ir** Iridium	78 **Pt** Platinum	79 **Au** Gold	80 **Hg** Mercury
87 **Fr** Francium	88 **Ra** Radium	Elements 89–103	104 **Rf** Rutherfordium	105 **Db** Dubnium	106 **Sg** Seaborgium	107 **Bh** Bohrium	108 **HS** Hassium	109 **Mt** Meitnerium	110 **Ds** Darmstadtium	111 **Rg** Roentgenium	112 **Cn** Copernicum

Atomic number — Chemical symbol

20 **Ca** Calcium — Name

57 **La** Lanthanum	58 **Ce** Cerium	59 **Pr** Praseodymium	60 **Nd** Neodymium	61 **Pm** Promethium	62 **Sm** Samarium	63 **Eu** Europium	64 **Gd** Gadolinium	65 **Tb** Terbium
89 **Ac** Actinium	90 **Th** Thorium	91 **Pa** Protactinium	92 **U** Uranium	93 **Np** Neptunium	94 **Pu** Plutonium	95 **Am** Americium	96 **Cm** Curium	97 **Bk** Berkelium

▶ Stars are made mainly of burning hydrogen, which is why they are so hot and bright.

▲ The Periodic Table is a chart of all the elements. In each row the atoms get heavier from left to right. Each column (up–down) contains elements with similar chemical features. Every element has a chemical symbol, name, and atomic number, which is the number of particles called protons in its central part, or nucleus.

75 Hydrogen is the simplest element and it is the first in the Periodic Table. This means it has the smallest atoms. It is a very light gas, which floats upwards in air. Hydrogen was used to fill giant airships. But there was a problem – hydrogen catches fire easily and explodes.

76 About 90 elements are found naturally on and in the Earth. In an element, all of its particles, called atoms, are exactly the same as each other. Just as important, they are all different from the atoms of any other element.

Note: Elements 113–118 are synthetic elements that have only been created briefly, so their properties cannot be known for certain.

13	14	15	16	17	18
					2 He Helium
5 B Boron	6 C Carbon	7 N Nitrogen	8 O Oxygen	9 F Fluorine	10 Ne Neon
13 Al Aluminium	14 Si Silicon	15 P Phosphorus	16 S Sulphur	17 Cl Chlorine	18 Ar Argon
31 Ga Gallium	32 Ge Germanium	33 As Arsenic	34 Se Selenium	35 Br Bromine	36 Kr Krypton
49 In Indium	50 Sn Tin	51 Sb Antimony	52 Te Tellurium	53 I Iodine	54 Xe Xenon
81 Ti Thallium	82 Pb Lead	83 Bi Bismuth	84 Po Polonium	85 At Astatine	86 Rn Radon
113 Uut Ununtrium	114 Uuq Ununquadium	115 Uup Ununpentium	116 Uuh Ununhexium	117 Uus Ununsectium	118 Uuo Ununoctium

66 Dy Dysprosium	67 Ho Holmium	68 Er Erbium	69 As Arsenic	70 Yb Ytterbium	71 Lu Lutetium
98 Cf Californium	99 Es Einsteinium	100 Fm Fermium	101 Md Mendelevium	102 No Nobelium	103 Lr Lawrencium

78 Uranium is a heavy and dangerous element. It gives off harmful rays and tiny particles. This process is called radioactivity and it can cause sickness, burns and diseases such as cancer. Radioactivity is a form of energy and, under careful control, radioactive elements are used as fuel in nuclear power stations.

▶ Aluminium is a strong but light metal that is ideal for forming the body of vehicles such as planes.

77 Carbon is a very important element in living things – including our own bodies. It joins easily with atoms of other elements to make large groups of atoms called molecules. When it is pure, carbon can be two different forms. These are soft, powdery soot, and hard, glittering diamond. The form depends on how the carbon atoms join to each other.

79 Aluminium is an element that is a metal, and it is one of the most useful in modern life. It is light and strong, it does not rust, and it is resistant to corrosion. Saucepans, drinks cans, cooking foil and jet planes are made mainly of aluminium.

Bond (link)   Atom

◀ Diamond is a form of the element carbon where the atoms are linked, or bonded, in a very strong box-like pattern.

Small science

80 Many pages in this book mention atoms. They are the smallest bits of a substance. They are so tiny, even a billion atoms would be too small to see. But scientists have carried out experiments to find out what's inside an atom. The answer is – even smaller bits. These are sub-atomic particles, and there are three main kinds.

81 At the centre of each atom is a blob called the nucleus. It contains two kinds of sub-atomic particles. These are protons and neutrons. Protons are positive, or plus. The neutron is neither positive nor negative. Around the centre of each atom are sub–atomic particles called electrons. They whizz round the nucleus. In the same way that a proton in the nucleus is positive or plus, an electron is negative or minus. The number of protons and electrons is usually the same.

82 Atoms of the various elements have different numbers of protons and neutrons. An atom of hydrogen has just one proton. An atom of helium, the gas put in party balloons to make them float, has two protons and two neutrons. An atom of the heavy metal called lead has 82 protons and 124 neutrons.

I DON'T BELIEVE IT!

One hundred years ago, people thought the electrons were spread out in an atom, like the raisins in a raisin pudding.

Hydrogen   Helium   Oxygen

▶ The bits inside an atom give each substance its features, from exploding hydrogen to life–giving oxygen.

• Electron
• Proton
• Neutron

83 It is hard to imagine the size of an atom. A grain of sand, smaller than this o, contains at least 100 billion billion atoms. If you could make the atoms bigger, so that each one becomes as big as a pin head, the grain of sand would be 2 kilometres high!

Electron

Nucleus made from protons and neutrons

Movement of electrons

84 'Nano' means one-billionth (1/1,000,000,000th), and nanotechnology is science at the smallest level – how atoms join to make molecules. It is fairly new, but it has already produced many useful products, from stronger materials in jet planes and racing cars, to self-cleaning glass and bouncier tennis balls!

▲ The protons and neutrons in the nucleus of an atom are held together by a powerful force.

◀ This idea for a nano gear-bearing allows the central axle to spin inside the outer collar. It could be used in micromachines.

▼ Buckyballs are ball-shaped structures made of carbon atoms, used in some types of solar panels and medical research.

▶ Like buckyballs, nanotubes are formed mainly of carbon atoms. They can be combined with plastics in hi-tech equipment such as racing bicycles.

Scientists at work

85 **There are thousands of different jobs and careers in science.** Scientists work in laboratories, factories, offices, mines, steelworks, nature parks and almost everywhere else. They find new knowledge and make discoveries using a process called the scientific method.

86 **First comes an idea, called a theory or hypothesis.** This asks or predicts what will happen in a certain situation. Scientists continually come up with new ideas and theories to test. One very simple theory is – if I throw a ball up in the air, will it come back down?

▲ Some scientific work involves handling microbes or dangerous chemicals. This means safety precautions such as wearing gloves and a face mask may be necessary.

▶ In scientific terms, throwing a ball into the air is an experiment. What will be the result?

QUIZ
Put these activities in the correct order, so that a scientist can carry out the scientific method.
1. Results 2. Experiment
3. Conclusions 4. Theory
5. Measurements

Answer: 4, 2, 5, 1, 3

87 **The scientist carries out an experiment or test, to check what happens.** The experiment is carefully designed and controlled, so that it will reveal useful results. Any changes are carried out one at a time, so that the effect of each change can be studied. The experiment for our simple theory is – throw the ball up in the air.

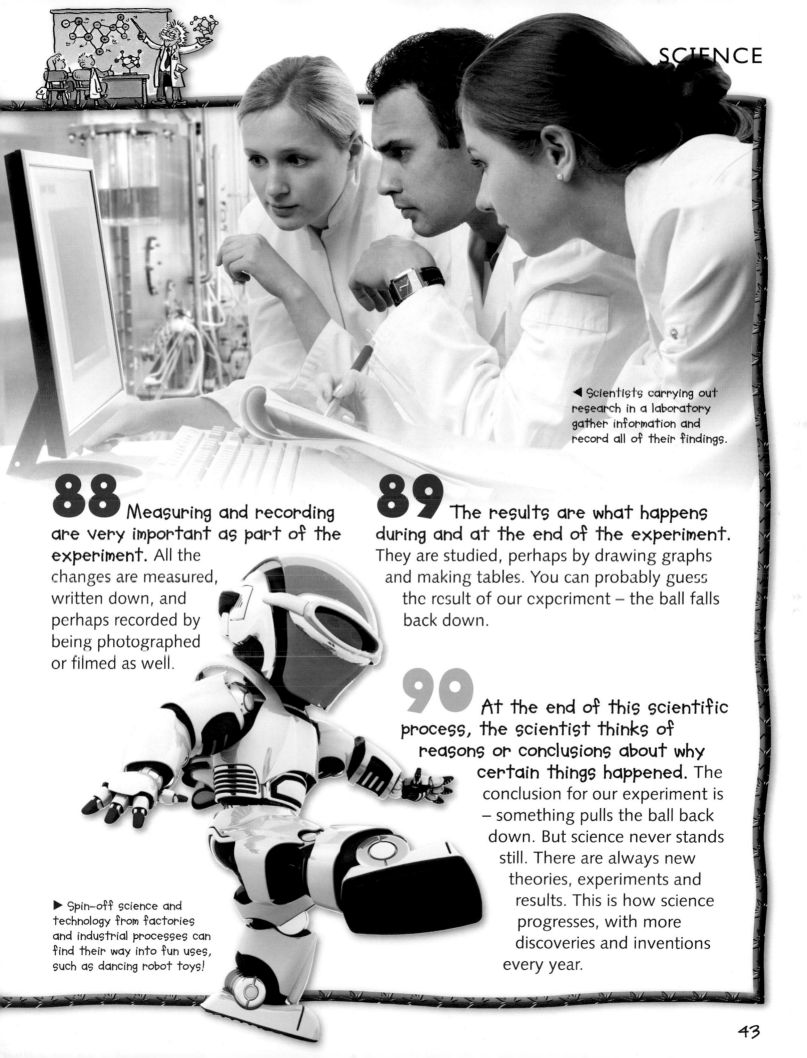

◄ Scientists carrying out research in a laboratory gather information and record all of their findings.

88 Measuring and recording are very important as part of the experiment. All the changes are measured, written down, and perhaps recorded by being photographed or filmed as well.

89 The results are what happens during and at the end of the experiment. They are studied, perhaps by drawing graphs and making tables. You can probably guess the result of our experiment – the ball falls back down.

90 At the end of this scientific process, the scientist thinks of reasons or conclusions about why certain things happened. The conclusion for our experiment is – something pulls the ball back down. But science never stands still. There are always new theories, experiments and results. This is how science progresses, with more discoveries and inventions every year.

► Spin-off science and technology from factories and industrial processes can find their way into fun uses, such as dancing robot toys!

Science in nature

91
Science and its effects are found all over the natural world. Scientists study living things such as animals and plants, as well as rocks and soil. They want to understand nature, and find out what effects science and its technology have on wildlife.

▼ One of the most important jobs in science is to study damage and pollution in the natural world. Almost everything we do affects wild places and animals and plants. For example, the power station here may make the river water warmer. This could encourage animals and plants accidentally introduced from tropical areas, which change the balance of nature.

92
One of the most complicated types of science is ecology. Ecologists try to understand how the natural world links together. They study how animals and plants live, what animals eat, and why plants grow better in some soils than others. They count the numbers of animals and plants and may trap animals briefly to study them, or follow the growth of trees in a wood. When the balance of nature is damaged, ecologists can help to find out why.

▼ The science of ecology involves long periods of studying nature in all kinds of habitats, from rivers to the seabed. For example, observing birds like herons, and fish such as trout, shows which foods they eat. This helps us to understand how changes to the habitat may affect them.

KEY

① Water beetle
② Rainbow trout
③ Water scorpion
④ Banded demoiselle damselfly
⑤ Heron
⑥ Otter
⑦ Warbler
⑧ Power station
⑨ Reedmace

◀ Oil spills and leaks cause vast damage to a region's ecology. Scientists advise on the best ways to clear up the pollution.

93 Ecologists use many forms of high–tech science in their studies. They may fit an animal with a radio-collar so that its movements can be tracked. Special cameras see in the dark and show how night hunters catch their prey. Radar used to detect planes can also follow flocks of birds. The sonar (echo-sounding) equipment of boats can track shoals of fish or whales.

◀ Tracking tigers is vital to know the threats faced by these endangered big cats, and help to save them.

Body science

94 One of the biggest areas of science is medicine. Medical scientists work to produce better drugs, more spare parts for the body and more machines for use by doctors. They also carry out scientific research to find out how people can stay healthy and prevent disease.

▲ Medical technology uses the latest equipment to diagnose illness, treat life-threatening conditions and cure diseases. This monitoring unit displays heart rate, pulse rate, amounts of oxygen in the blood, breathing speed, blood pressure and other vital signs.

95

As parts of the body work, such as the muscles and nerves, they produce tiny pulses of electricity. Pads on the skin pick up these pulses, which are displayed as a wavy line on a screen or paper strip. The ECG (electro-cardiograph) machine shows the heart beating. The EEG (electro-encephalograph) shows nerve signals flashing around the brain.

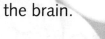
Laser beam hits retina inside eye

▶ A laser beam shines safely through the front of the eye to mend inner problems such as a detached retina.

MAKE A PULSE MACHINE

You will need:
modelling clay   drinking straw

Find your pulse by feeling your wrist, just below the base of your thumb, with a finger of the other hand. Place some modelling clay on this area, and stick a drinking straw into it. Watch the straw twitch with each heartbeat. Now you can see and feel your pulse. Check your pulse rate by counting the number of heartbeats in one minute.

96

Laser beams are ideal for delicate operations, or surgery, on body parts such as the eye. The beam makes very small, precise cuts. It can be shone into the eye and made most focused, or strongest, inside. So it can make a cut deep within the eye, without any harm to the outer parts.

▶ An endoscope is inserted into the body to give a doctor a picture on screen. The treatment can be given immediately.

97

The endoscope is like a flexible telescope made of fibre-strands. This is pushed into a body opening such as the mouth, or through a small cut, to see inside. The surgeon looks into the other end of the endoscope, or at a picture on a screen.

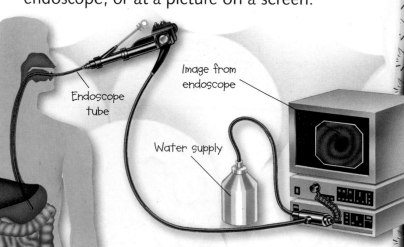

Endoscope tube

Image from endoscope

Water supply

Science in the future

98 **Many modern machines and processes can cause damage to our environment and our health.** The damage includes acid rain, destruction of the ozone layer and the greenhouse effect, leading to climate change and global warming. Science can help to find solutions. New filters and chemicals called catalysts can reduce dangerous fumes from vehicle exhausts and power stations, and in the chemicals in factory waste pipes.

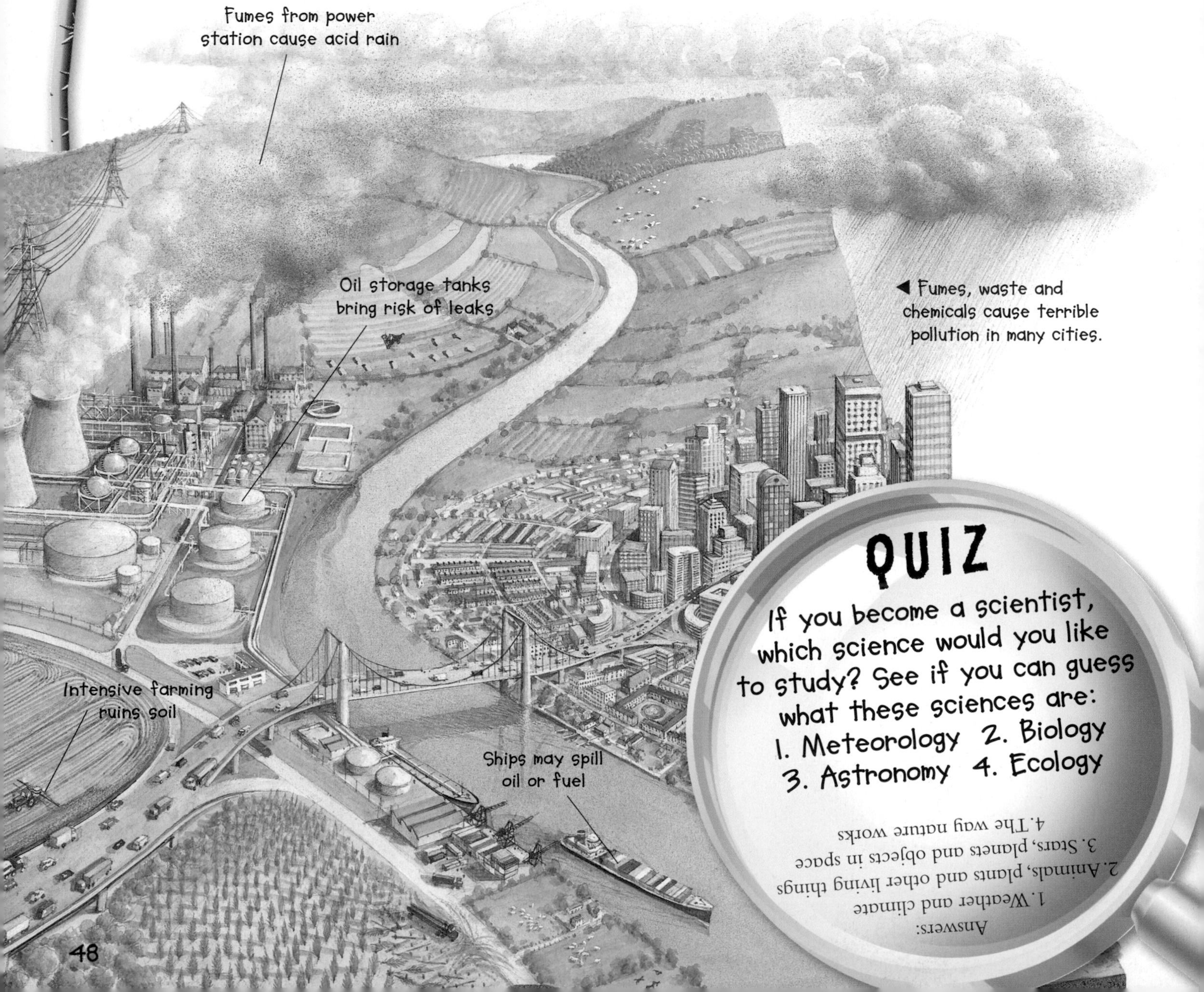

Fumes from power station cause acid rain

Oil storage tanks bring risk of leaks

◀ Fumes, waste and chemicals cause terrible pollution in many cities.

Intensive farming ruins soil

Ships may spill oil or fuel

QUIZ

If you become a scientist, which science would you like to study? See if you can guess what these sciences are:
1. Meteorology 2. Biology
3. Astronomy 4. Ecology

Answers:
1. Weather and climate
2. Animals, plants and other living things
3. Stars, planets and objects in space
4. The way nature works

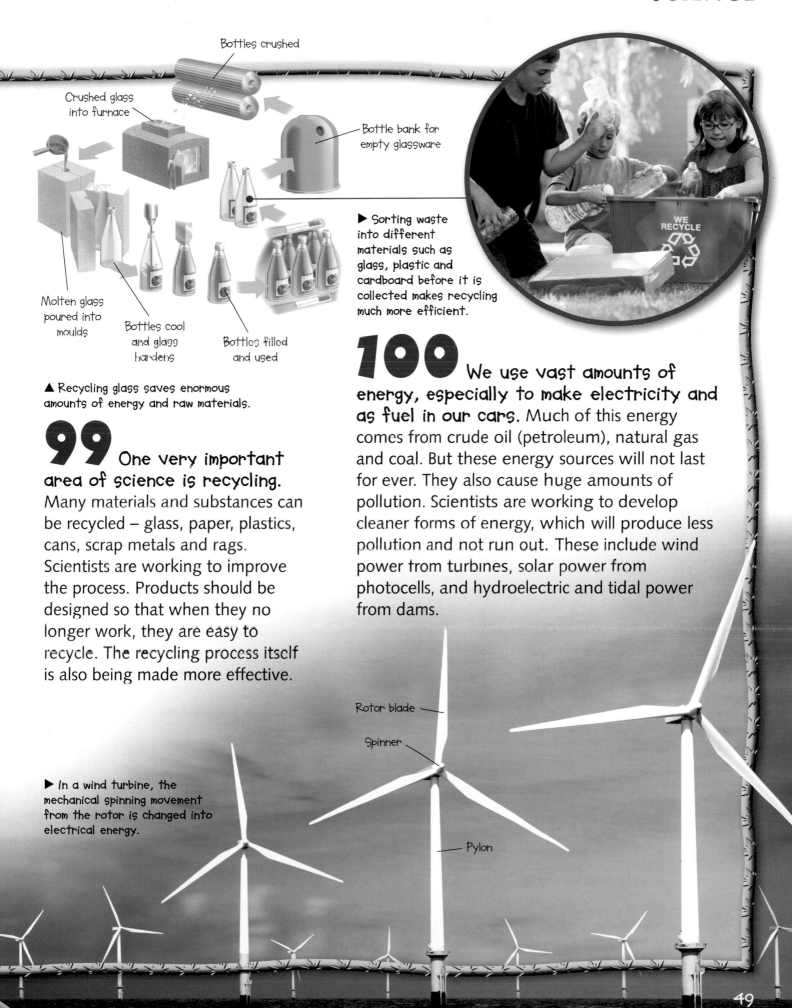

Bottles crushed

Crushed glass into furnace

Bottle bank for empty glassware

Molten glass poured into moulds

Bottles cool and glass hardens

Bottles filled and used

▲ Recycling glass saves enormous amounts of energy and raw materials.

▶ Sorting waste into different materials such as glass, plastic and cardboard before it is collected makes recycling much more efficient.

99 One very important area of science is recycling.

Many materials and substances can be recycled – glass, paper, plastics, cans, scrap metals and rags. Scientists are working to improve the process. Products should be designed so that when they no longer work, they are easy to recycle. The recycling process itself is also being made more effective.

100 We use vast amounts of energy, especially to make electricity and as fuel in our cars.

Much of this energy comes from crude oil (petroleum), natural gas and coal. But these energy sources will not last for ever. They also cause huge amounts of pollution. Scientists are working to develop cleaner forms of energy, which will produce less pollution and not run out. These include wind power from turbines, solar power from photocells, and hydroelectric and tidal power from dams.

Rotor blade

Spinner

Pylon

▶ In a wind turbine, the mechanical spinning movement from the rotor is changed into electrical energy.

SPACE

101 **Space is all around Earth, high above the air.** Here on Earth we are surrounded by air. If you go upwards – for example, by climbing a high mountain or flying in a plane – the air grows thinner until there is none at all. Space officially begins 100 kilometres up from sea level. It is mostly empty, but there are many exciting things such as planets, stars and galaxies. People who travel in space are called astronauts.

▶ In space, astronauts wear spacesuits to go outside a space station or a spacecraft as it circles Earth. Much farther away are planets, stars and galaxies.

Our life-giving star

102 **The Sun is our nearest star.** Most stars are so far away they look like points of light in the sky. The Sun looks different because it is much closer to us. Unlike Earth, which is solid, the Sun is a ball of super-hot gases – so hot that they glow like the flames of a bonfire.

◀ The Sun's hot, glowing gas is always on the move, bubbling up to the surface and sinking back down again.

103 **Nothing could live on Earth without the Sun.** Deep in its centre the Sun is constantly making energy that keeps its gases hot and glowing. This energy works its way to the surface where it escapes as heat and light. Without it, Earth would be cold and dark with no life at all.

PROMINENCE

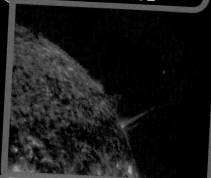

Solar prominences can reach temperatures of 10,000°C.

SOLAR FLARE

Solar flares erupt in a few minutes, then take more than half an hour to die away again.

SUNSPOT

Groups of sunspots seem to move across the Sun over two weeks, as the Sun rotates.

104 **The Sun is often spotty.** Sunspots appear on the surface, some wider than Earth. They look dark because they are cooler than the rest of the Sun. Solar flares – explosions of energy – can suddenly shoot out from the Sun. The Sun also throws huge loops of gas called prominences out into space.

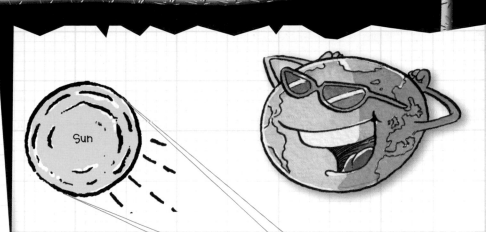

▶ When the Moon casts a shadow on Earth, there is a solar eclipse.

Sun

Moon

Earth

Total eclipse

▲ A photo of a solar eclipse on 1 August 2008 shows the Moon totally blocking the Sun, and reveals the Sun's halo-like corona – part of its atmosphere not normally seen because the Sun's surface is too bright.

105 **When the Moon hides the Sun there is a solar eclipse.** Every so often, the Sun, Moon and Earth line up in space so that the Moon comes directly between the Earth and the Sun. This stops the sunlight from reaching a small area on Earth. This area grows dark and cold, as if night has come early.

I DON'T BELIEVE IT!
The surface of the Sun is nearly 60 times hotter than boiling water. It is so hot it would melt a spacecraft flying near it.

WARNING
Never look directly at the Sun, especially not through a telescope or binoculars. It is so bright it will harm your eyes and could even make you blind.

A family of planets

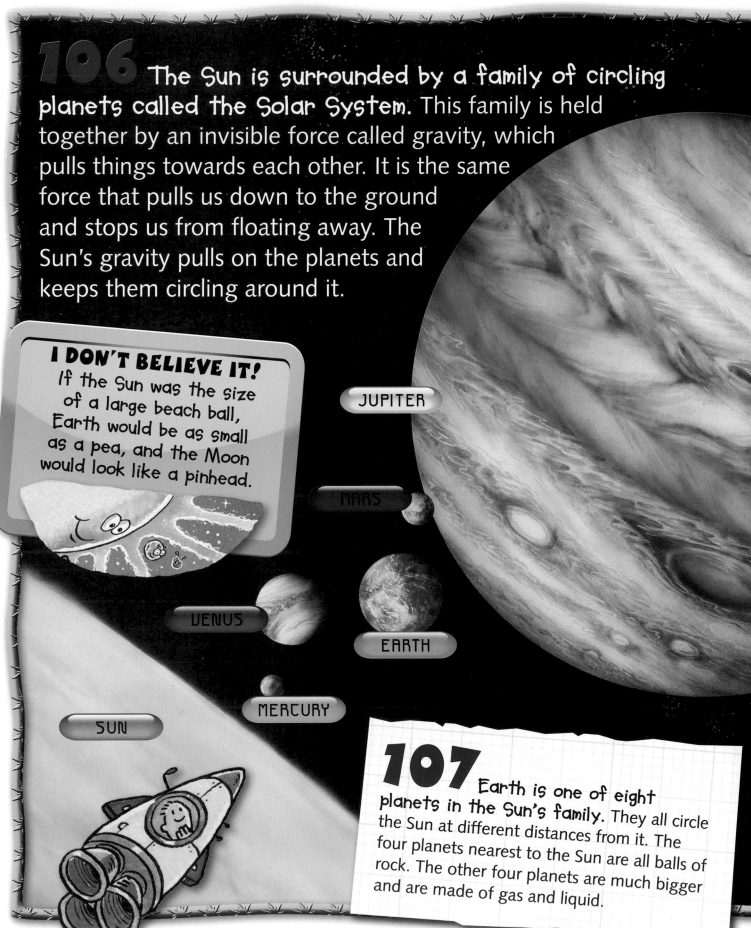

106 The Sun is surrounded by a family of circling planets called the Solar System. This family is held together by an invisible force called gravity, which pulls things towards each other. It is the same force that pulls us down to the ground and stops us from floating away. The Sun's gravity pulls on the planets and keeps them circling around it.

I DON'T BELIEVE IT!
If the Sun was the size of a large beach ball, Earth would be as small as a pea, and the Moon would look like a pinhead.

JUPITER

MARS

VENUS

EARTH

MERCURY

SUN

107 Earth is one of eight planets in the Sun's family. They all circle the Sun at different distances from it. The four planets nearest to the Sun are all balls of rock. The other four planets are much bigger and are made of gas and liquid.

▼ The eight planets are all different. Mercury, nearest the Sun, is small and hot. Then Venus, Earth and Mars are rocky and cooler. Beyond them Jupiter, Saturn, Uranus and Neptune are large and cold.

NEPTUNE

URANUS

SATURN

108
Moons circle the planets, travelling with them round the Sun. Earth has one moon. It circles Earth while Earth circles round the Sun. Mars has two tiny moons, but Mercury and Venus have none at all. There are large families of moons, like miniature solar systems, around all the large gas planets.

109
There are millions of smaller members in the Sun's family. Some are tiny specks of dust speeding through space between the planets. Larger chunks of rock, many as large as mountains, are called asteroids. Comets come from the edge of the Solar System, skimming past the Sun before they disappear again.

Planet of life

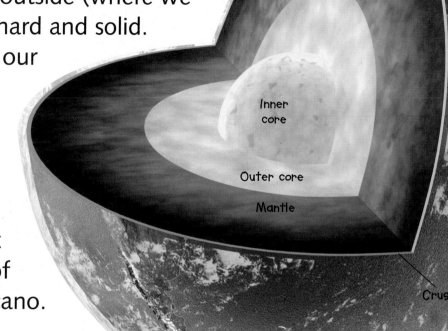

Inner core

Outer core

Mantle

Crust

Atmosphere

110 **The planet we live on is called Earth.** It is a round ball of rock. On the outside (where we live) the rock is hard and solid. But deep below our feet, inside the Earth, the rock is hot enough to melt. You can sometimes see this hot rock showering out of an erupting volcano.

▶ Earth's inner core is made of iron. It is very hot and keeps the outer core as liquid. Outside this is the mantle, made of thick rock. The thin surface layer that we live on is called the crust.

▼ No other planet in the Solar System has liquid water on its surface, so Earth is the only known planet suitable for life.

111 **Earth is the only planet with life.** From space, Earth is a blue-and-white planet, with huge oceans and wet masses of cloud. Animals – including people – and plants can live on Earth because of all this water.

112 Sunshine gives us daylight when it is night on the other side of the Earth. When it is daytime, your part of the Earth faces towards the Sun and it is light. At night, your part faces away from the Sun and it is dark. Day follows night because the Earth is always turning.

As Earth rotates, the day and night halves shift gradually around the world. Earth turns eastwards, so the Sun rises in the east as each part of the world spins to face it.

I DON'T BELIEVE IT!

The Moon has no air. When astronauts went to the Moon they had to take air with them in their spacecraft and spacesuits.

114 Craters on the Moon are scars from space rocks crashing into its surface. When a rock smashes into the Moon at high speed, it leaves a saucer-shaped dent, pushing some of the rock outwards into a ring of mountains.

113 The Moon seems to change shape. Over a month it changes from a thin crescent to a round shape. This is because sunlight is reflected by the Moon. We see the full Moon when the sunlit side faces Earth and a thin, crescent shape when most of the sunlit side is facing away from us.

Crescent moon

Half moon

Full moon

Half moon

Crescent moon

▲ During the first half of each monthly cycle, the Moon waxes (appears to grow). During the second half, it wanes (dwindles) back to a crescent-shape.

▲ Dark patches are called seas although there is no water on the Moon.

The Earth's neighbours

115 Venus and Mars are the nearest planets to Earth. Venus is closer to the Sun than Earth while Mars is farther away. Each takes a different amount of time to circle the Sun and we call this its year. A year on Venus is 225 days, on Earth 365 days and on Mars 687 days.

116 Venus is the hottest planet, even though Mercury is closer to the Sun. Heat builds up on Venus because it is completely covered by clouds that trap the heat, like the glass in a greenhouse.

▲ Dense clouds surround Venus, making it difficult to observe, so the *Magellan* spacecraft spent four years mapping the surface with radar (bouncing radio waves) to produce images like this.

▲ Under its clouds, Venus has hundreds of volcanoes, large and small, all over its surface. We do not know if any of them are still erupting.

117 The clouds around Venus are poisonous — they contain drops of acid that would burn your skin. They are not like clouds on Earth, which are made of droplets of water. They are thick, and do not let much sunshine reach the surface of Venus.

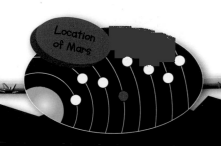

Location of Mars

118

Winds on Mars whip up huge dust storms that can cover the whole planet. Mars is very dry, like a desert, and covered in red dust. When a space probe called *Mariner 9* arrived there in 1971, the whole planet was hidden by dust clouds.

Camera

Radio aerial

Solar panel

▲ *Mariner 9* was the first space probe to circle another planet. Since that time more than 30 other crafts have travelled there and several have soft-landed.

119

Mars has the largest volcano in the Solar System. It is called Olympus Mons and is three times as high as Mount Everest, the tallest mountain on Earth. Olympus Mons is an old volcano and it has not erupted for millions of years.

LIFE ON MARS

Mars is the best known planet besides Earth. It is dry, rocky and covered in dust. Look in books and on the Internet to find out more about Mars. What do you think it would be like to live there?

120

There are plans to send astronauts to Mars but the journey would take six months or more. The astronauts would have to take with them everything they need for the journey there and back and for their stay on Mars.

◄ The Hubble Space Telescope has captured a giant dust storm in this picture of Mars. The bright orange patch in the middle shows where the dry red dust is blown up by strong winds.

The smallest of all

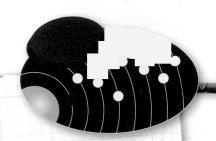

121 Mercury looks like our Moon. It is a round, cratered ball of rock. Although a little larger than the Moon, like the Moon it has no air.

MAKE CRATERS
You will need:
flour   baking tray
a marble or a stone

1. Spread some flour about 2 centimetres deep on a baking tray and smooth over the surface.
2. Drop a marble or a small round stone onto the flour.
3. Can you see the saucer-shaped crater the marble makes?

◀ Mercury has high cliffs and long ridges as well as craters. Astronomers think it cooled and shrank in the past, making its surface wrinkled.

122 The sunny side of Mercury is boiling hot but the night side is freezing cold. Being the nearest planet to the Sun, the sunny side can get twice as hot as an oven. But Mercury spins round slowly so the night side has time to cool down, and there is no air to trap the heat. The night side becomes more than twice as cold as Antarctica – the coldest place on Earth.

CRATERS

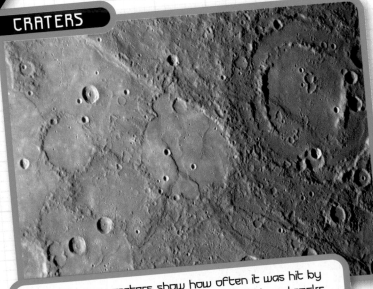

Mercury's many craters show how often it was hit by space rocks. One was so large that it shattered rocks on the other side of the planet.

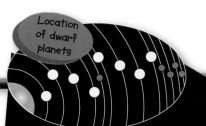

Location of dwarf planets

123 Tiny, rocky Pluto was discovered in 1930. At first it was called a planet, but in 2006, it was re-classified as a dwarf planet. It is less than half the width of Mercury. In fact, Pluto is smaller than our Moon.

124 Aside from Pluto, four other dwarf planets have been named. They are called Ceres, Eris, Makemake and Haumea (in order from the closest to the Sun to the farthest away). Eris is larger than Pluto.

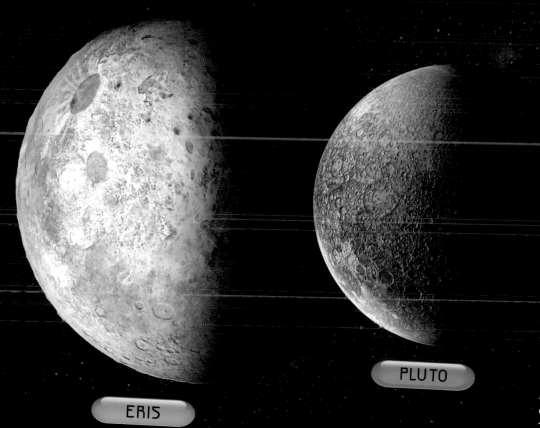

ERIS

PLUTO

CERES

▲ Ceres orbits between Mars and Jupiter. Pluto orbits further away from the Sun than Neptune, and Eris is further out still.

125 If you stood on the surface of Pluto, the Sun would not look much brighter than any other stars. Pluto is so far from the Sun that it receives little heat and is completely covered in ice.

126 The first space probe to visit Pluto will be *New Horizons*. It blasted off in 2006 and is due to reach the dwarf planet by 2015. If all goes well it will then carry on to the outer region of the Solar System, called the Kuiper Belt.

The biggest of all

127 Jupiter is more massive than the other seven planets in the Solar System put together. It is 11 times as wide as Earth, although it is still much smaller than the Sun. Saturn, the next largest planet, is more than nine times as wide as the Earth.

128 Jupiter has more than 60 moons. Its moon Io has many active volcanoes that throw out huge plumes of material, making red blotches and dark marks on its orange-yellow surface.

129 The Great Red Spot on Jupiter is a 300-year-old storm. It was first noticed about 300 years ago and is at least twice as wide as the Earth. It rises above the rest of the clouds and swirls around like storm clouds on Earth.

◄ Jupiter's fast winds blow clouds into coloured bands around the planet.

▼ There are many storms on Jupiter but none are as large or long-lasting as the Great Red Spot.

Io

Europa

Ganymede

Callisto

These four large moons were discovered by Galileo Galilei in 1610, which is why they are known as the Galilean moons.

▶ Although Saturn's rings are very wide, they stretch out in a very thin layer around the planet.

130
The shining rings around Saturn are made of millions of chunks of ice. These circle the planet like tiny moons and shine by reflecting sunlight from their surfaces. Some are as small as ice cubes while others are as large as a car.

131
Jupiter and Saturn are gas giants. They have no solid surface for a spacecraft to land on. All that you can see are the tops of their clouds. Beneath the clouds, the planets are made mostly of gas (like air) and liquid (water is a liquid).

▼ Taken with the Hubble Space Telescope, this image shows a detailed view of Saturn's southern hemisphere and its rings.

I DON'T BELIEVE IT!
For its size, Saturn is lighter than any other planet. If there was a large enough sea, it would float like a cork.

132
Jupiter and Saturn spin round so fast that they bulge out in the middle. This can happen because they are not made of solid rock. As they spin, their clouds are stretched out into light and dark bands around them.

So far away

▲ This photo shows an aurora display (the glowing blue dot) on Uranus. Aurorae are made by tiny particles given off by the Sun, known as the solar wind. These get trapped by a planet's magnetism and start to glow.

133 Uranus and Neptune are gas giants like Jupiter and Saturn. They are the next two planets beyond Saturn but are much smaller, being less than half as wide. They too have no hard surface. Their cloud tops make Uranus and Neptune both look blue. They are very cold, being so far from the Sun.

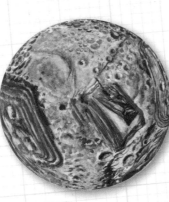

► Uranus's moon Miranda looks as though it has been split apart and put back together again.

134 Uranus seems to 'roll' around the Sun. Most of the other planets spin upright like tops, but Uranus spins on its side. It may have been knocked over when something crashed into it millions of years ago.

▼ Uranus's five largest moons are big enough to be classified as dwarf planets, but they are not in direct orbit of the Sun.

	NAME	DIAMETER	YEAR OF DISCOVERY
1	Titania	1578 km	1787
2	Oberon	1523 km	1787
3	Umbriel	1169 km	1851
4	Ariel	1158 km	1851
5	Miranda	472 km	1948

135 Uranus has more than 25 moons, and there are probably more to be discovered. Most are very small, but Titania, the largest, is 1578 kilometres across, which makes it the eighth largest moon in the Solar System.

Location of Neptune

136

Neptune had a storm that disappeared. When the *Voyager 2* space probe flew past Neptune in 1989 it spotted a huge storm, like a dark version of the Great Red Spot on Jupiter. But when the Hubble Space Telescope looked at Neptune in 1994, the storm had gone.

▲ *Voyager 2* is the only probe to visit Neptune and send back close up pictures of the planet.

137

Neptune has bright blue clouds that make the whole planet look blue. Above them are smaller white streaks – icy clouds that race around the planet. One of these clouds, seen by the *Voyager 2* space probe, was named 'Scooter' because it scooted around the planet so fast.

QUIZ

1. How many moons does Uranus have?
2. When was Uranus's moon Miranda discovered?
3. Which planet seems to 'roll' around the Sun?
4. What colour are Neptune's clouds?

Answers:
1. More than 25 2. 1948
3. Uranus 4. Blue

138

Neptune is sometimes farther from the Sun than Pluto. Planets and dwarf planets go around the Sun on orbits (paths) that look like circles, but Pluto's path is more squashed. This sometimes brings it closer to the Sun than Neptune.

Orbit of Pluto

Sun

Neptune

Pluto

Orbit of Neptune

▲ Neptune is so far from the Sun that its orbit lasts 164.79 Earth years. It has only completed one orbit since it was discovered in 1846.

139 There are probably billions of tiny comets at the edge of the Solar System. They circle the Sun far beyond Neptune. Sometimes one is disturbed and moves inwards towards the Sun, looping around it before going back to where it came from. Some comets come back to the Sun regularly – Halley's comet returns every 76 years.

The solid part of a comet is hidden inside a huge, glowing cloud that stretches into a long tail.

140 A comet is often called a dirty snowball because it is made of dust and ice mixed together. Heat from the Sun melts some of the ice. This makes dust and gas stream away from the comet, forming a huge tail that glows in the sunlight.

141 Comet tails always point away from the Sun. Although it looks bright, a comet's tail is extremely thin so it is blown outwards, away from the Sun. When the comet moves away from the Sun, its tail goes in front of it.

142 Asteroids are chunks of rock that failed to stick together to make a planet. Most of them circle the Sun between Mars and Jupiter where there would be room for another planet. There are millions of asteroids, some the size of a car, and others as big as mountains.

ASTEROIDS

Asteroids travel in a ring around the Sun. This ring is called the asteroid belt and can be found between Mars and Jupiter.

143 Meteors are sometimes called shooting stars. They are not really stars, just streaks of light that flash across the night sky. Meteors are made when pebbles racing through space at high speed hit the top of the air above the Earth. The pebble gets so hot it burns up. We see it as a glowing streak for a few seconds.

▼ This crater in Arizona is one of the few large meteorite craters visible on Earth. The Moon is covered in them.

QUIZ

1. Which way does a comet tail always point?
2. What is another name for a meteor?
3. Where is the asteroid belt?

Answers:
1. Away from the Sun
2. Shooting star
3. Between Mars and Jupiter

A star is born

144 Stars are born in clouds of dust and gas called nebulae. Astronomers can see these clouds as shining patches in the night sky, or dark patches against the distant stars. These clouds shrink as gravity pulls the dust and gas together. At the centre, the gas gets hotter and hotter until a new star is born.

145 Stars begin their lives when they start making energy. When the dust and gas pulls tightly together it gets very hot. Finally it gets so hot in the middle that it can start making energy. The energy makes the star shine, giving out heat and light like the Sun.

QUIZ

1. What is a nebula?
2. How long has the Sun been shining?
3. What colour are large hot stars?
4. What is a group of new young stars called?

Answers:
1. A cloud of dust and gas in space 2. About 4.6 billion years 3. Bluish-white 4. Star cluster

KEY

1 Clumps of gas in a nebula start to shrink into the tight round balls that will become stars. The gas spirals round as it is pulled inwards.

2 Deep in its centre, the new star starts making energy, but it is still hidden by the cloud of dust and gas.

3 The dust and gas are blown away and we can see the star shining. Any left over gas and dust may form planets around the new star.

146

Young stars often stay together in clusters. When they start to shine they light up the nebula, making it glow with bright colours. Then the starlight blows away the remains of the cloud and we can see a group of new stars, called a star cluster.

STAR CLUSTER

This cluster of young stars, with many stars of different colours and sizes, will gradually drift apart, breaking up the cluster.

147

Large stars are very hot and white, smaller stars are cooler and redder. A large star can make energy faster and get much hotter than a smaller star. This gives them a very bright, bluish-white colour. Smaller stars are cooler. This makes them look red and shine less brightly. Ordinary in-between stars – like our Sun – look yellow.

148

Smaller stars live much longer than huge stars. Stars use up their gas to make energy, and the largest stars use up their gas much faster than smaller stars. The Sun is about halfway through its life. It has been shining for about 4.6 billion years and will go on shining for another 5 billion years.

(2)

(3)

Death of a star

149 Stars begin to die when they run out of gas to make energy. The middle of the star begins to shrink but the outer parts expand, making the star much larger.

At the end of their lives stars swell up into red giant stars, as shown in this far infrared image, or even larger red supergiants.

150 Red giant stars are dying stars that have swollen to hundreds of times their normal size. Their expanding outer layers get cooler, making them look red. When the Sun is a red giant it will be large enough to swallow up the nearest planets, Mercury and Venus, and perhaps Earth.

151 Eventually, a red giant's outer layers drift away, making a halo of gas around the star. The starlight makes this gas glow and we call it a planetary nebula. All that is left is a small, hot star called a white dwarf, which cannot make energy and gradually cools and dies.

PLANETARY NEBULA

This bow-tie shaped nebula is made by material cast off by a dying star as it enters its white dwarf phase.

WHITE DWARF STARS

These ancient white dwarf stars are in our Milky Way Galaxy, and are between 12 and 13 billion years old.

152 Very heavy stars end their lives in a huge explosion called a supernova. This explosion blows away all the outer parts of the star. All that is left is a tiny hot star in the middle of a shell of hot glowing gas.

▶ Cassiopeia A is one of the best-studied supernova remnants. This image was made using data from three different types of telescopes.

I DON'T BELIEVE IT!
One of the main signs of a black hole is radiation from very hot gases near one just before they are sucked in.

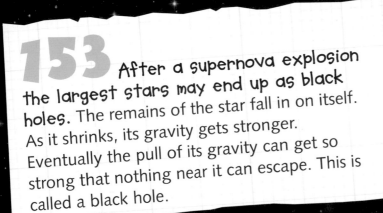

153 After a supernova explosion the largest stars may end up as black holes. The remains of the star fall in on itself. As it shrinks, its gravity gets stronger. Eventually the pull of its gravity can get so strong that nothing near it can escape. This is called a black hole.

▲ Hot gas falling into a black hole called Cygnus X-1 gives out powerful X-rays picked up by the Chandra satellite.

154 The Sun is part of a huge family of stars called the Milky Way Galaxy. There are billions of other stars in our galaxy, as many as the grains of sand on a beach. We call it the Milky Way because it looks like a very faint band of light in the night sky, as though someone has spilt some milk across space.

▶ With binoculars you can see that the faint glow of the Milky Way comes from millions of stars in our galaxy.

155 Curling arms give some galaxies their spiral shape. The Milky Way has arms made of bright stars and glowing clouds of gas that curl round into a spiral shape. Some galaxies, called elliptical galaxies, have a round shape like a squashed ball. Other galaxies have no particular shape.

I DON'T BELIEVE IT!
If you could fit the Milky Way onto these two pages, the Sun would be so tiny, you could not see it.

A CLUSTER OF GALAXIES

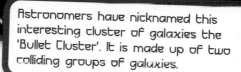

156 There are billions of galaxies outside the Milky Way. Some are larger than the Milky Way and many are smaller, but they all have more stars than you can count. The galaxies tend to stay together in groups called clusters.

Astronomers have nicknamed this interesting cluster of galaxies the 'Bullet Cluster'. It is made up of two colliding groups of galaxies.

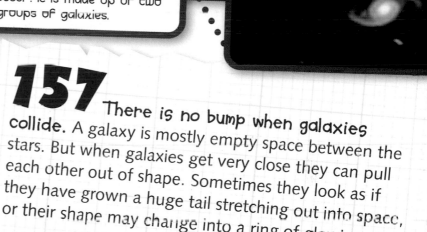

ELLIPTICAL

SPIRAL

IRREGULAR

▲ Galaxies can be categorized by their shape. The Milky Way is a spiral galaxy.

157 There is no bump when galaxies collide. A galaxy is mostly empty space between the stars. But when galaxies get very close they can pull each other out of shape. Sometimes they look as if they have grown a huge tail stretching out into space, or their shape may change into a ring of glowing stars.

▲ These two galaxies are so close that each has pulled a long tail of bright stars from the other.

What is the Universe?

158 The Universe is the name we give to everything we know about. This means everything on Earth, from tiny bits of dust to the highest mountain, and everything that lives here. It also means everything in space – all the billions of stars in the billions of galaxies.

159 The Universe started with a massive explosion called the Big Bang. Astronomers think that this happened about 13.7 billion years ago. The explosion sent everything racing outwards in all directions. To start with, everything was packed incredibly close together. Over time it has expanded (spread out) into the Universe we can see today, which is mostly empty space.

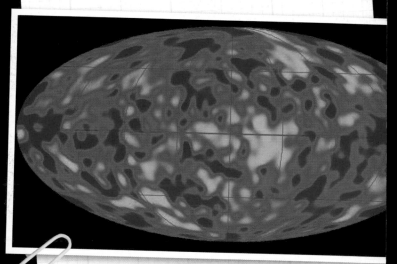

▲ A satellite has measured and mapped the oldest light in the Universe, known as the cosmic microwave background, providing a snapshot of the early Universe.

160 The Universe's matter includes planets, stars and gas, and its energy includes light and heat. Scientists suspect that it also contains unknown dark matter and dark energy, which we are unable to detect. These may affect what finally happens to the Universe.

DARK MATTER

Some of the distant galaxies in this cluster appear distorted, because light coming from them is being bent by invisible dark matter.

161
The galaxies are still racing away from each other. When astronomers look at distant galaxies they can see that other galaxies are moving away from our galaxy, and the more distant galaxies are moving away faster. In fact all the galaxies are moving apart from each other. We say that the Universe is expanding.

DOTTY UNIVERSE
You will need:
balloon   pen
Blow up a balloon a little, holding the neck to stop air escaping. Mark dots on the balloon with a pen, then blow it up some more. Watch how the dots move apart from each other. This is like the galaxies moving apart as the Universe expands.

162
We do not know what will happen to the Universe billions of years in the future. It may keep on expanding. If this happens, old stars will gradually die and no new ones will be born. Everywhere will become dark and cold.

KEY

1 All the parts that make up the Universe were once packed tightly together. No one knows why the Universe started expanding with a Big Bang.

2 As everything moved apart in all directions, stars and galaxies started to form.

3 Today there are galaxies of different shapes and sizes, all moving apart. One day they may start moving towards each other.

4 The Universe could stop expanding, or shrink and end with a Big Crunch.

Looking into space

163 People have imagined they can see the outlines of people and animals in the star patterns in the sky. These patterns are called constellations. Hundreds of years ago astronomers named the constellations to help them find their way around the skies.

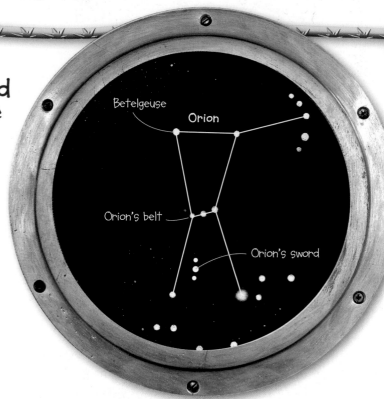

▲ The constellation Orion (shown here in the Northern Hemisphere) is one of the most recognizable in the night sky.

◄ The constellation Scorpius (in the Southern Hemisphere) is easy to recognize because it looks like a scorpion with a curved tail.

164 Astronomers use huge telescopes to see much more than we can see with just our eyes. Telescopes make things look bigger and nearer. They also show faint, glowing clouds of gas, and distant stars and galaxies.

▲ Mauna Kea observatory is situated on the summit of Mauna Kea on the US island of Hawaii. Telescopes are usually located high up, far from towns and cities so that they have a clear view of the skies.

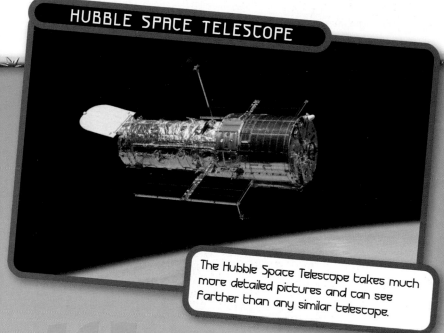

HUBBLE SPACE TELESCOPE

The Hubble Space Telescope takes much more detailed pictures and can see farther than any similar telescope.

166 Space telescopes look even further to find exciting things in deep space. On Earth, clouds often hide the stars and the air is always moving, which blurs the pictures made by the telescopes. A telescope in space above the air can make clearer pictures. The Hubble Space Telescope has been circling the Earth for more than 20 years and sending back beautiful pictures.

165 Astronomers also look at radio signals from space. Radio telescopes look like huge satellite TV dishes. They make pictures using radio signals that come from space. The pictures do not always look like those from ordinary telescopes, but they can spot things that most ordinary telescopes cannot see, such as jets of gas from black holes.

MOON WATCH

You will need:
binoculars

On a clear night look at the Moon through binoculars, holding them very steady. You will be able to see the round shapes of craters. Binoculars are really two telescopes, one for each eye, and they make the Moon look bigger so you can see more detail.

◀ Radio telescopes often have rows of dishes like these to collect radio signals from space. Together, they act like one much larger dish to make more detailed pictures. The dishes can move to look in any direction.

Three, two, one... Lift-off!

167 A rocket must travel over 40 times faster than a jumbo jet to blast into space. Slower than that, and gravity will pull it back to Earth. Rockets are powered by burning fuel, which makes hot gases. These gases rush out of the engines, shooting the rocket upwards.

◄ Each stage fires its engine to make the rocket go faster and faster until it puts the satellite into space.

Second stage
This needs less power and fuel to keep it going

Fuel tank

Oxidizer tank

First stage
This uses its fuel and then falls away, otherwise it would be 'dead weight'

Rocket engine

The shuttle was blasted into space by three rocket engines and two huge booster rockets.

168 A single rocket is usually not powerful enough to launch a satellite or spacecraft. So most have two or three stages, which are really separate rockets mounted on top of each other, each with its own engines. When the first stage has used up its fuel it drops away, and the second stage starts. Finally the third stage takes over to go into space.

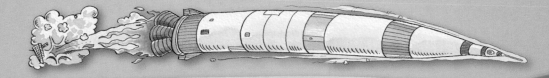

169 **Some launchers have boosters.** These are extra rockets fixed to the main one. Most boosters burn solid fuel, like giant firework rockets. They fall away when the fuel has burnt up. Some drift down on parachutes into the sea, to be used again.

The shuttle puts down its wheels and lands on the runway. A parachute and speed brakes bring the shuttle to a standstill.

◀ On 8 July, 2011, space shuttle *Atlantis* took off from Florida, USA on the final mission of the 30-year space shuttle programme.

The space shuttles were re-usable spaceplanes. There were more than 130 missions, starting in 1981. The shuttle took off straight up like a rocket, carrying a load of up to 24 tonnes. To land, it swooped down to glide onto a runway.

Living in space

SPACE WALK

171 **Space is a dangerous place for astronauts.** It can be boiling hot in the sunshine or freezing cold in the Earth's shadow. There is also dangerous radiation from the Sun. Dust, rocks and bits from other rockets race through space at such speed, they could easily make a small hole in a spacecraft, letting the air leak out.

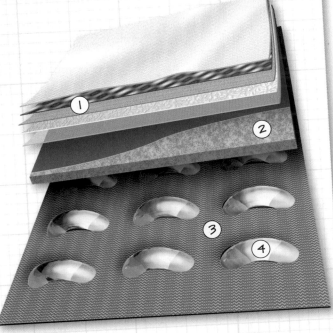

▼ In a spacesuit, many layers of different materials are needed to keep the astronaut safe.

KEY

❶ Outer layers protect the wearer from the fierce heat of the Sun

❷ This layer seals the suit from the vacuum of space

❸ Soft lining goes next to the skin

❹ Tubes carrying cooling water

It is not easy for an astronaut wearing a bulky spacesuit to hold tools or bend his or her arms.

172 Spacesuits protect astronauts when they are out in space. They are very bulky because they are made of many layers to make them strong. They must hold the air for astronauts to breathe and protect them against speeding dust and harmful radiation. To keep the astronauts cool while they work outside the spacecraft, tubes of water under the spacesuit carry away heat.

SPACE MEALS

You will need:

dried noodles   boiling water

Buy a dried snack such as noodles, which just needs boiling water added. This is the kind of food astronauts eat. Most of their meals are dried so they are not too heavy to launch into space.

174 **Everything floats around in space as if it has no weight.** So all objects have to be fixed down or they will float away. Astronauts have footholds to keep them still while they are working. They strap themselves into sleeping bags so they don't bump into things when they are asleep.

173 **Astronauts must take everything they need into space with them.** Out in space there is no air, water or food, so all the things that astronauts need to live must be packed into their spacecraft and taken with them.

▶ Sleeping bags are fixed to walls so astronauts look as though they are asleep standing up.

Home from home

175 A space station is a home in space for astronauts and cosmonauts (Russian astronauts). It has a kitchen for making meals, and cabins with sleeping bags. There are toilets, wash basins and sometimes showers. There are places to work, and controls where astronauts can check that everything is working properly.

▼ The International Space Station provides astronauts with a home in space. It is still being constructed whilst in orbit.

176 Sixteen countries are helping to build the International Space Station (ISS) in space. These include the US, Russia, Japan, Canada, Brazil and 11 European countries. It is built up from separate sections called modules that have been made to fit together like a jigsaw.

I DON'T BELIEVE IT!
The US space station *Skylab*, launched in 1973, fell back to Earth in 1979. Most of it landed in the ocean but some pieces hit Australia.

KEY
❶ Solar panels for power
❷ Space shuttle
❸ Docking port
❹ Control module
❺ Living module
❻ Soyuz ferry

An aerial view of a hurricane swirling on Earth is captured by an ISS crew member in September 2010.

177 Each part is launched from Earth and added to the ISS in space. There they are fitted by astronauts at the ISS with the help of a robot arm. Huge panels of solar cells have been added. These turn sunlight into electricity to provide a power supply for the space station.

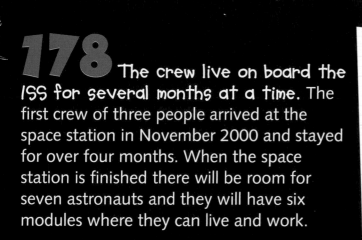

178 The crew live on board the ISS for several months at a time. The first crew of three people arrived at the space station in November 2000 and stayed for over four months. When the space station is finished there will be room for seven astronauts and they will have six modules where they can live and work.

179 People and supplies can travel to the ISS in Russian Soyuz spacecraft. There are also robot ferries with no crew, including Russian Progress craft and European ATVs (Automated Transfer Vehicles). In 2001, American Dennis Tito became the first space tourist, staying on the ISS for eight days.

Robot explorers

180 Robot spacecraft called probes have explored all the planets. Probes take close-up pictures and measurements, and send the data back to scientists on Earth. Some probes circle planets taking pictures. For a really close-up look, a probe can land on the surface.

181 In 1976, two Viking spacecraft landed on Mars to look for life. They scooped up some dust and tested it to see if any tiny creatures lived on Mars. They did not find any signs of life and their pictures showed only a dry, red, dusty desert.

Cameras

Power supply

▶ Voyager 2 gave us close-up pictures of four different planets.

Radio dish sends messages to Earth

182 Two Voyager probes left Earth in 1977 to visit the gas giant planets. They reached Jupiter in 1979, flying past and on to Saturn. *Voyager 2* then went on to visit Uranus in 1986 and Neptune in 1989. They sent back thousands of close-up pictures of each planet and its moons and rings as they flew past. They also discovered new rings and many new moons around the giant planets. Both Voyagers are now leaving the Solar System and will send back information about space between the stars until 2020.

◀ The Viking landers took soil samples from Mars, but found no signs of life.

183 The *Galileo* space probe arrived at Jupiter in 1995 and circled the planet for nearly 8 years. It found that two of its largest moons may have watery oceans hidden under their thick icy surfaces. *Juno* will be the next probe to visit Jupiter, aiming to find out more about how the giant planet formed.

▲ The *Juno* space probe will arrive at Jupiter in 2016 and circle the planet studying its deep swirling clouds.

▶ Called *Spirit* and *Opportunity*, the rovers are 2.3 metres wide and 1.5 metres tall to the cameras on their masts.

184 In 2003, two rockets launched the twin Mars Exploration Rovers (MERs) — remote-controlled robot vehicles. They landed on Mars in January 2004, and trundled around, taking pictures and gathering data. Another rover, named *Curiosity*, touched down in 2012 to search for evidence that Mars once supported life.

QUIZ

1. When did the Voyager probes fly past Jupiter?
2. How long did the *Galileo* probe circle Jupiter?
3. Which probes tested the dust on Mars for signs of life?
4. How tall are *Spirit* and *Opportunity*?

Answers:
1. 1979 2. 8 years
3. Viking 4. 1.5 metres

85

Watching the Earth

185 **Hundreds of satellites circle the Earth in space.** They are launched into space by rockets and may stay there for ten years or more.

187 **Communications satellites carry TV programmes and telephone messages around the world.** Large aerials on Earth beam radio signals up to a space satellite that then beams them down to another aerial, half way round the world. This lets us talk to people on the other side of the world, and watch events such as the Olympics Games while they are happening in faraway countries.

▼ Weather satellites look down at the clouds and give warning when a violent storm is approaching.

▼ Communications satellites can beam TV programmes directly to your home through your own aerial dish.

186 **Weather satellites help the forecasters tell us what the weather will be like.** These satellites can see where the clouds are forming and which way they are going. They watch the winds and rain and measure how hot the air and the ground are.

▶ The different satellites each have their own job to do, looking at the Earth, or the weather, or out into space.

▶ Satellite telescopes let astronomers look far out into the Universe and discover what is out there.

▼ Pictures of the Earth taken by satellites can help make very accurate maps.

188 **Earth-watching satellites look out for pollution.** Oil slicks in the sea and dirty air over cities show up clearly in pictures from these satellites. They can help farmers by showing how well crops are growing and by looking for pests and diseases. Spotting forest fires and icebergs that may be a danger to ships is also easier from space.

189 **Satellite telescopes let astronomers look at exciting things in space.** They can see other kinds of radiation as well as light. For example, X-ray telescopes can tell astronomers where there may be a black hole.

Voyage to the Moon

190 The first men landed on the Moon in 1969. They were two astronauts from the US Apollo 11 mission. Neil Armstrong was the first person to set foot on the Moon. Only five other Apollo missions have landed on the Moon since then.

191 The giant *Saturn 5* rocket launched the astronauts on their journey to the Moon. It was the largest rocket to have ever been built. Its three stages lifted the astronauts into space, and the third stage gave it an extra boost to send it to the Moon.

▲ In 1969, about half a billion people watched U.S. astronaut Neil Armstrong's first steps onto another world.

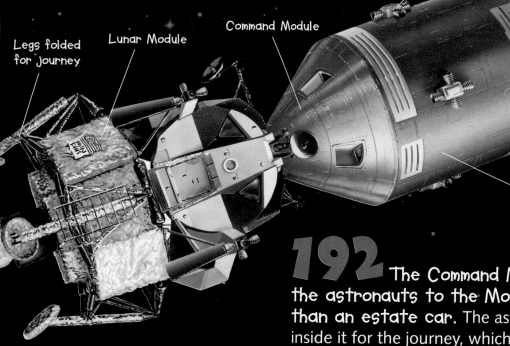

Thrusters

Legs folded for journey

Lunar Module

Command Module

Main engine

Service Module with fuel and air supplies

▲ The Lunar and Command Modules travelled to the Moon fixed together, then separated for the Moon landing.

192 The Command Module that carried the astronauts to the Moon had no more room than an estate car. The astronauts were squashed inside it for the journey, which took three days to get there and another three to get back. On their return, the Command Module, with the astronauts inside, splashed down in the sea.

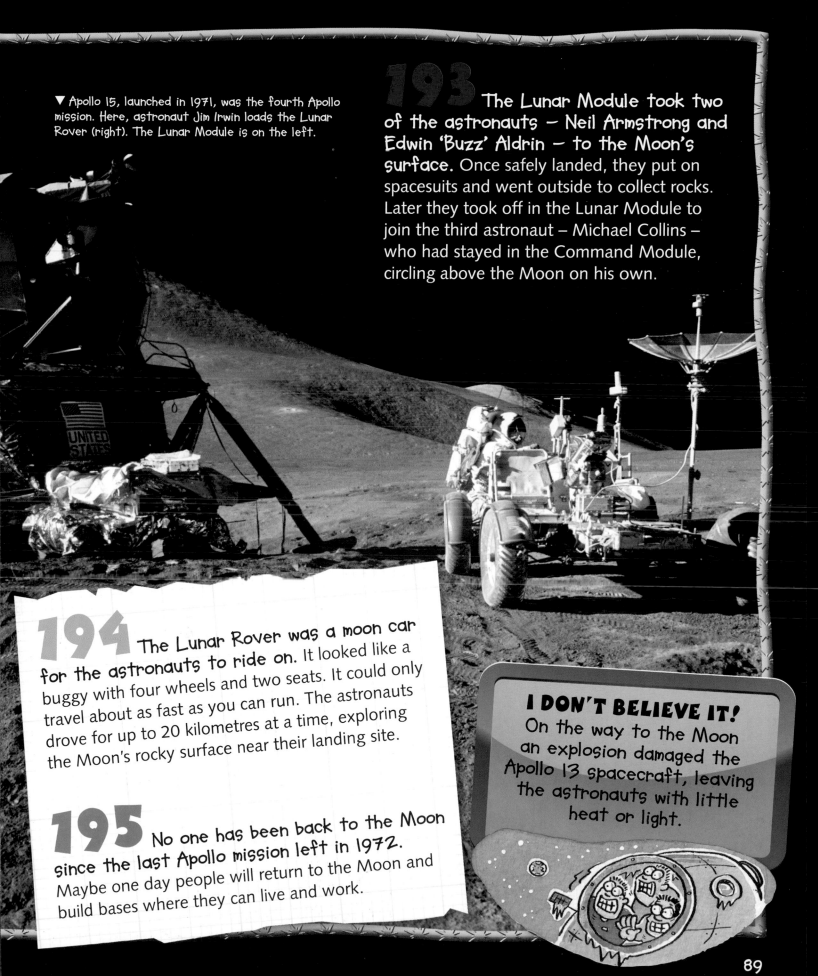

▼ Apollo 15, launched in 1971, was the fourth Apollo mission. Here, astronaut Jim Irwin loads the Lunar Rover (right). The Lunar Module is on the left.

193 **The Lunar Module took two of the astronauts – Neil Armstrong and Edwin 'Buzz' Aldrin – to the Moon's surface.** Once safely landed, they put on spacesuits and went outside to collect rocks. Later they took off in the Lunar Module to join the third astronaut – Michael Collins – who had stayed in the Command Module, circling above the Moon on his own.

194 **The Lunar Rover was a moon car for the astronauts to ride on.** It looked like a buggy with four wheels and two seats. It could only travel about as fast as you can run. The astronauts drove for up to 20 kilometres at a time, exploring the Moon's rocky surface near their landing site.

195 **No one has been back to the Moon since the last Apollo mission left in 1972.** Maybe one day people will return to the Moon and build bases where they can live and work.

I DON'T BELIEVE IT!
On the way to the Moon an explosion damaged the Apollo 13 spacecraft, leaving the astronauts with little heat or light.

Are we alone?

196 The only life we have found so far in the Universe is here on Earth. Everywhere you look on Earth from the frozen Antarctic to the hottest, driest deserts, on land and in the sea, there are living things. Some are huge, such as whales and elephants, and others are much too small to see. But they all need water to live.

▼ On Earth, animals can live in a wide range of different habitats, such as in the sea, in deserts and jungles, and icy lands.

DESERT

SEA

POLAR LANDS

RAINFOREST

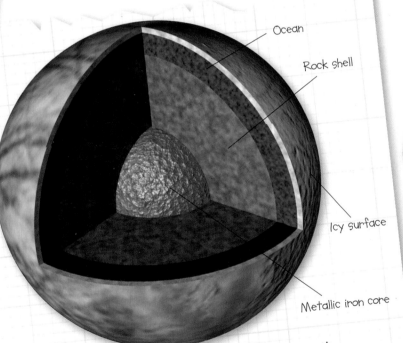

Ocean

Rock shell

Icy surface

Metallic iron core

▲ Deep beneath Europa's cracked, icy surface, it may be warm enough for the ice to melt into water.

197 There may be an underground ocean on Europa, one of Jupiter's moons. Europa is a little smaller than our Moon and is covered in ice. However, astronomers think that there may be an ocean of water under the ice. If so, there could be strange living creatures swimming around deep underground.

▲ No one knows what other exoplanets would be like. They could have strange moons or colourful rings. Anything that lives there might look very strange to us.

198 Astronomers have found planets circling other stars, called exoplanets. Most of them are large, like Jupiter. But perhaps some could be smaller, like Earth. They could have a rocky surface that is not too hot or too cold, and suitable for liquid water – known as 'Goldilocks planets' after the fairytale character who tried the three bears' porridge. These planets could support some kind of life.

199 Mars seems to have had rivers and seas billions of years ago. Astronomers can see dry riverbeds and ridges that look like ocean shores on its surface. This makes them think Mars may have been warm and wet long ago and something may once have lived there. Now it is very cold and dry with no sign of life.

I DON'T BELIEVE IT!
It would take thousands of years to get to the nearest stars with our present spacecraft.

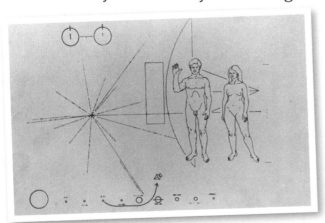

▲ Maybe the Pioneer plaques will be found by aliens who perhaps can read them and come to visit us!

200 Each Pioneer probe carries a plaque about 23 centimetres wide. They show pictures of a man and woman, with the Solar System along the bottom and a chart of where the Earth is among the stars. In space the Pioneers will keep going forever, unless they hit something like a moon, a planet or an asteroid.

WEATHER

201 Rain, sunshine, snow and storms are all types of weather. Different weather is caused by what is happening in the atmosphere – the air around us and above our heads. In some parts of the world, the weather changes every day, but in others, it is nearly always the same. Weather affects how animals, plants and people survive and behave.

▼ This map shows the different types of climate that are found in different places around the world.

EUROPE

NORTH
AMERICA

AFRICA

Equator

Cold temperate
Cold winter with snow,
cool dry summer

SOUTH
AMERICA

Wet temperate
Cool winter, warm summer,
rain all year round

Mountainous
Gets steadily colder
as land gets higher

Temperate grassland
Cold winter with snow,
hot, dry summer

Tropical forest
Hot and rainy all
year round

Polar
Sub–zero temperatures
and snow all year round

Desert
Hot in day, cold at night,
very little rain

ASIA

OCEANIA

Dry temperate
Mild winter with rain,
hot dry summer

ANTARCTICA

Tropical
Hot all year round
with seasonal rain

▲ Different colours on the map indicate different types
of climate. In general, the warmest climates are found close
to the Equator. The closer to the Poles – the two points
at opposite ends of the Earth – the cooler the climate.

202 Tropical, temperate and
polar are all types of climate. Climate is
the name we give to patterns of weather
over a period of time. Near the Equator (an
imaginary belt around the middle of the
Earth), the weather is mostly hot
and steamy. We call this a
tropical climate. Near the
North and South Poles,
ice lies on the ground
all year round and there
are biting-cold blizzards.
This is a polar climate. Most of
the world has a temperate climate – a mix
of cold and warm seasons.

93

Four seasons

203 The reason we have seasons lies in space. Due to the pull of the Sun's gravity, Earth is on a continuous path through space that takes it around the Sun. This path, or orbit, takes one year. The Earth is tilted, so over the year first one and then the other Pole leans towards the Sun, giving us seasons. In June, for example, the North Pole is tilted towards the Sun. The Sun heats the northern half of the Earth and it is summer.

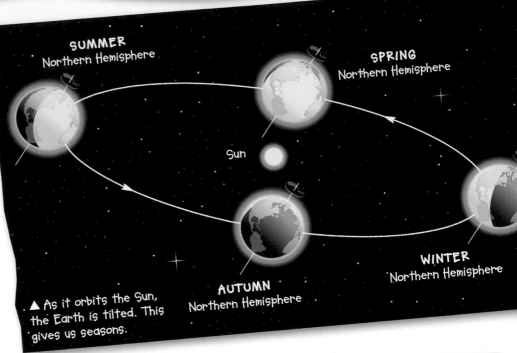

SUMMER
Northern Hemisphere

SPRING
Northern Hemisphere

Sun

AUTUMN
Northern Hemisphere

WINTER
Northern Hemisphere

▲ As it orbits the Sun, the Earth is tilted. This gives us seasons.

204 When it is summer in Argentina, it is winter in Canada. In December, the South Pole leans towards the Sun. Places in the southern half of the world, such as Argentina, have summer. At the same time, places in the northern half, such as Canada, have winter.

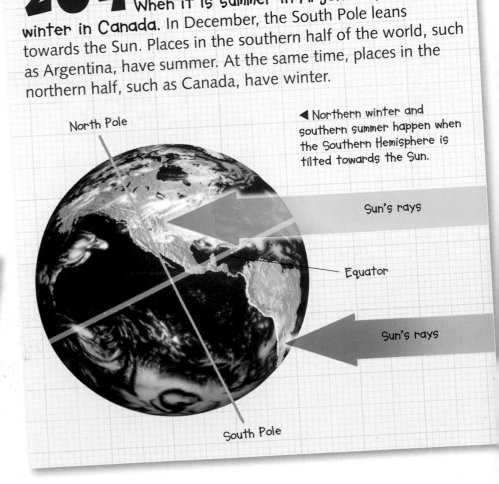

North Pole

◄ Northern winter and southern summer happen when the Southern Hemisphere is tilted towards the Sun.

Sun's rays

Equator

Sun's rays

South Pole

I DON'T BELIEVE IT!
When the Sun shines all day in the far north, there is 24-hour night in the far south.

▼ Near the North Pole, the Sun never sets below the horizon on Midsummer's Day.

205 A day can last 21 hours! Night and day happen because Earth is spinning as it circles the Sun. At the height of summer, places near the North Pole are so tilted towards the Sun that it is light almost all day long. In Stockholm, Sweden on Midsummer's Eve, daytime lasts for 21 hours because the Sun disappears below the horizon for only three hours.

▶ Trees that lose their leaves in autumn are called deciduous. Evergreens are trees that keep their leaves all year round.

AUTUMN

Leaves change colour and start to fall. Fruits ripen.

WINTER

Branches are bare.

SUMMER

Flowering trees are in full bloom. Some have a second growth spurt.

SPRING

Leaf buds start to grow. The leaves soon open and flowers bloom.

206 Some forests change colour in the autumn. Autumn comes between summer and winter. Trees prepare for the cold winter months ahead by losing their leaves. First, though, they suck back the precious green chlorophyll, or dye, in their leaves, making them turn glorious shades of red, orange and brown.

Fewer seasons

▲ When monsoon rains are especially heavy, they can cause chaos. Streets turn to rivers and sometimes people's homes are washed away.

207 Monsoons are winds that carry heavy rains. The rains fall in the tropics in summer during the hot, rainy season. The Sun warms up the sea, which causes huge banks of cloud to form. Monsoons then blow these clouds towards land. Once the rains hit the continent, they can pour for weeks.

POTENTIAL FLASH FLOOD AREAS

NEXT 6 MILES

◀ This sign warns of flash flooding in California, USA.

208 Monsoons happen mainly in Asia. However, there are parts of the Americas, close to the Equator, that also have a rainy season. Winds can carry heavy rain clouds, causing flash floods in the southwestern deserts of the USA. The floods happen because the land has been baked hard during the dry season so water doesn't drain away.

209 Many parts of the tropics have two seasons, not four. They are the parts of the world closest to the Equator. Here it is always hot, as these places are constantly facing the Sun. However, the Earth's movement affects the position of a great band of cloud. In June, the tropical areas north of the Equator have the strongest heat and the heaviest rainstorms. In December, it is the turn of the areas south of the Equator.

Tropic of Cancer

Equator

Tropic of Capricorn

▲ The tropics lie either side of the Equator, between lines of latitude called the Tropic of Cancer and the Tropic of Capricorn.

◄ Daily rainfall feeds lush rainforest vegetation and countless waterfalls in the mountains of Costa Rica.

210 Tropical rainforests have rainy weather all year round. There is usually about 2000 millimetres of rainfall in a year. Rainforests still have a wet and a dry season, but the wet season is even wetter! Some parts of the rainforest can become flooded during the wet season, as the heavy rain makes rivers overflow their banks.

What a scorcher!

211 All of our heat comes from the Sun. The Sun is a star, a super-hot ball of burning gases. It gives off heat rays that travel 150 million kilometres through space to reach Earth. During the journey, the rays cool down, but they are still hot enough to scorch the Earth.

212 The Sahara is the sunniest place on Earth. This North African desert once had 4300 hours of sunshine in a year! People who live here, such as the Tuareg Arabs, cover their skin to avoid being sunburnt.

► Desert peoples wear headdresses to protect their skin and eyes from the sun and sand.

213 The hottest temperature on Earth was measured at Death Valley in California, USA. An air temperature of 56.7°C was recorded in 1913. Al Aziziyah in Libya had held a record of 58°C for 90 years, but in 2012 this was reanalyzed and found to be incorrect.

214

The Sun can trick your eyes. Sometimes, as sunlight passes through our atmosphere, it hits layers of air at different temperatures. When this happens, the air bends the light and can trick our eyes into seeing something that is not there. This is a mirage. For example, what looks like a pool of water might really be part of the sky reflected on to the land.

▲ A mirage is just a trick of the light. It can make us see something that is not really there.

215

Too much sun brings drought. Clear skies and sunshine are not always good news. Without rain, crops wither, and people and their animals go hungry.

216

One terrible drought made a 'Dust Bowl'. Settlements in the American Midwest were devestated by a long drought during the 1930s. As crops died, there were no roots to hold the soil together. The dry earth turned to dust and some farms simply blew away!

▼ During the 1930s, dust storms caused by drought in Oklahoma, USA covered fields in layers of dust.

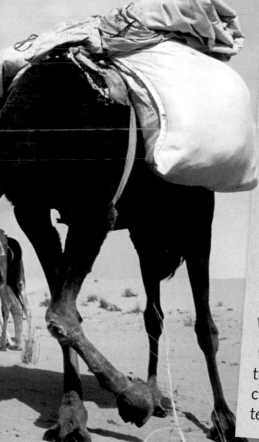

Warm water

OCEANIA

PACIFIC OCEAN

SOUTH AMERICA

▲ El Niño has been known to cause violent weather conditions. It returns on average every four years.

Cold water

217

A sea current can set forests alight. All sorts of things affect our weather and climate. The movements of a sea current called El Niño have been blamed for causing flooding and terrible droughts – which can lead to unstoppable forest fires.

Our atmosphere

218 Our planet is wrapped in a blanket of air. We call this blanket the atmosphere. It stretches hundreds of kilometres above our heads. The atmosphere keeps in heat, especially at night when part of the planet faces away from the Sun. During the day, it becomes a sunscreen instead, protecting us from the Sun's fierce rays. Without an atmosphere, there would be no weather.

219 Most weather happens in the troposphere. This is the layer of atmosphere that stretches from the ground to around 10 kilometres above your head. The higher in the troposphere you go, the cooler the air. Because of this, clouds are most likely to form here. Clouds with flattened tops show just where the troposphere meets the next layer, the stratosphere.

KEY

1. Exosphere
   190 to 960 kilometres
2. Thermosphere
   80 to 190 kilometres
3. Mesosphere
   50 to 80 kilometres
4. Stratosphere
   10 to 50 kilometres
5. Troposphere
   0 to 10 kilometres

Low-level satellites orbit within the exosphere

The Northern and Southern Lights – the auroras – are formed in the thermosphere

Meteors entering the amosphere burn up in the mesosphere, causing 'shooting stars'

Aeroplanes either fly high in the troposphere, or in the lower levels of the stratosphere

Weather forms in the troposphere

► This view of the Earth from the International Space Station, which orbits the Earth, shows the atmosphere as a thin, wispy layer.

▲ The atmosphere stretches right into space. Scientists have split it into five layers, or spheres.

220

Air just cannot keep still. Tiny particles in air, called molecules, are always bumping into each other. The more they do this, the greater the air pressure. Generally, there are more collisions lower in the troposphere, because the pull of gravity makes the molecules fall towards the Earth's surface. The higher you go, the lower the air pressure, and the less oxygen there is in the air.

221

Warmth makes air move. When heat from the Sun warms the molecules in air, they move faster and spread out more. This makes the air lighter, so it rises in the sky, creating low pressure. As it gets higher, the air cools. The molecules slow down and become heavier again, so they start to sink back to Earth.

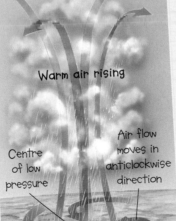

HIGH PRESSURE

LOW PRESSURE

Cool air sinking

Warm air rising

Centre of high pressure

Air flow moves in clockwise direction

Centre of low pressure

Air flow moves in anticlockwise direction

▲ A high pressure weather system gives us warmer weather, while low pressure gives us cooler, more unsettled weather. (In the Northern Hemisphere, air flows anticlockwise in a low pressure system, and clockwise in high pressure. In the Southern Hemisphere, it is the opposite.)

▲ At high altitudes there is less oxygen. That is why mountaineers often wear breathing equipment.

Clouds and rain

222 **Rain comes from the sea.** As the Sun heats the surface of the ocean, some seawater turns into water vapour and rises into the air. As it rises, it cools and turns back into water droplets. Lots of water droplets make clouds. The droplets join together to make bigger and bigger drops that eventually fall as rain. Some rain is soaked up by the land, but a lot finds its way back to the sea. This is called the water cycle.

KEY	
①	Water evaporates from the sea
②	Clouds form
③	Water is given off by trees
④	Rain falls, filling rivers
⑤	Rivers run back to the sea

223 **Some mountains are so tall that their summits (peaks) are hidden by cloud.** They can even affect the weather. When moving air hits a mountain slope it is forced upwards. As it travels up, the temperature drops, and clouds form.

▼ The peak of Chapaeva, in the Tian Shan mountain range in Asia, can be seen above the clouds.

WARM AIR

▼ Water moves in a continuous cycle between the ocean, atmosphere and land.

224 Clouds release energy.
When water vapour becomes water droplets and forms clouds, a small amount of heat energy is given out into the atmosphere. Then, when the droplets fall as rain, kinetic, or movement, energy is released as the rain hits the ground.

RAIN GAUGE

You will need:
jam jar   waterproof marker pen
ruler   notebook   pen

Put the jar outside. At the same time each day, mark the rainwater level on the jar with your pen. At the end of a week, empty the jar. Measure and record how much rain fell each day and over the whole week.

▶ Virga happens when rain reaches a layer of dry air. The rain droplets turn back into water vapour in mid–air, and seem to disappear.

225 Some rain never reaches the ground.
The raindrops turn back into water vapour because they hit a layer of super-dry air. You can actually see the drops falling like a curtain from the cloud, but the curtain stops in mid-air. This type of weather is called virga.

Not just fluffy

226 **Clouds come in all shapes and sizes.** Scientists divide clouds into three basic types – cirrus, stratus, and cumulus – according to their shape and height above the ground. Cirrus clouds look like wisps of smoke. They form high in the troposphere and rarely mean rain. Stratus clouds form in flat layers and may produce drizzle or a sprinkling of snow. Most types of cumulus clouds bring rain. They look soft and fluffy.

227 **Not all cumulus clouds produce rain.** Cumulus humilis clouds are the smallest heap-shaped clouds. In the sky, they look like lumpy, cotton wool sausages! They are too small to produce rain but they can grow into much bigger, rain-carrying cumulus clouds. The biggest cumulus clouds, called cumulonimbus, bring heavy rainfall.

Cirrus
Thin, wispy high-level clouds, sometimes called 'mare's tails'

Cumulonimbus
Towering grey-white clouds that produce heavy rainfall

Cumulus
Billowing clouds with flat bases

Nimbostratus
Dense layer of low, grey rain clouds

▶ The main classes of cloud – cirrus, cumulus and stratus – were named in the 1800s. An amateur British weather scientist called Luke Howard identified the different types.

Cirrocumulus
Ripples or rows of small
white clouds at high altitude

Contrails
The white streaks
created by planes

Altocumulus
Small globular clouds
at middle altitude

228 **Not all clouds are made by nature.** Contrails are streaky clouds that a plane leaves behind it as it flies. They are made of water vapour that comes from the plane's engines. The second it hits the cold air, the vapour turns into ice crystals, leaving a trail of white cloud.

Altostratus
Layered grey middle–level
cloud with no visible holes

229 Sometimes the sky is filled with white patches of cloud that look like shimmering fish scales. These are called mackerel skies. It takes lots of gusty wind to break the cloud into these little patches, and so mackerel skies are usually a sign of changeable weather.

Stratocumulus
Grey clouds in patches or
globules that may join together

◄ A mackerel sky over Calanais stone circle in Scotland.

Stratus
Continuous low cloud near,
but not touching, the ground

Flood warning

230 **Too much rain brings flooding.** There are two different types of floods. Flash floods happen after a short burst of heavy rainfall, usually caused by thunderstorms. Broadscale flooding happens when rain falls steadily over a wide area – for weeks or months – without stopping. When this happens, rivers slowly fill and eventually burst their banks. Tropical storms, such as hurricanes, can also lead to broadscale flooding.

▲ The power of flood water has caused great damage to this house in Australia.

231 **There can be floods in the desert.** When a lot of rain falls very quickly on to land that has been baked dry, it cannot soak in. Instead, it sits on the surface, causing flash floods.

▼ A desert flash flood in the Grand Canyon, USA, has created streams of muddy water. After the water level falls, vegetation will burst into life.

I DON'T BELIEVE IT!

The ancient Egyptians had a story to explain the yearly flooding of the Nile. They said the goddess Isis filled the river with tears, as she cried for her lost husband.

232

There really was a Great Flood. The Bible tells of a terrible flood, and how a man called Noah was saved. Recently, explorers found the first real evidence of the flood – a sunken beach 140 metres below the surface of the Black Sea. There are ruins of houses, dating back to 5600 BC. Stories of a flood in ancient times do not only appear in the Bible – the Babylonians and Greeks told of one, too.

▼ In the Bible, Noah survived the Great Flood by building a huge wooden boat called an ark.

233

Mud can flood. When rain mixes with earth it makes mud. On bare mountainsides, there are no tree roots to hold the soil together. An avalanche of mud can slide off the mountain. The worst ever mudslide happened after flooding in Colombia, South America in 1985. It buried 23,000 people from the town of Armero.

◄ Torrential rain in Brazil caused this mudslide, which swept away part of a village.

Deep freeze

▶ This truck has become stuck in a snow drift. Falling snow is made worse by strong winds, which can form deep drifts.

234 Snow is made of tiny ice crystals. When air temperatures are very cold – around 0°C – the water droplets in the clouds freeze to make tiny ice crystals. Sometimes, individual crystals fall, but usually they clump together into snowflakes.

▼ A snowflake that is several centimetres across will be made up of lots of crystals, like these.

235 No two snowflakes are the same. This is because snowflakes are made up of ice crystals, and every ice crystal is as unique as your fingerprint. Most crystals look like six-pointed stars, but they come in other shapes too.

236 Black ice is not really black. Drizzle or rain turns to ice when it touches freezing-cold ground. This 'black' ice is see-through, and hard to spot against a road's dark tarmac. It is also very slippery, creating dangerous driving conditions.

I DON'T BELIEVE IT!
Antarctica is the coldest place on Earth. Temperatures of −89.2°C have been recorded there.

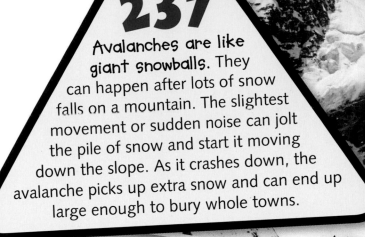

237

Avalanches are like giant snowballs. They can happen after lots of snow falls on a mountain. The slightest movement or sudden noise can jolt the pile of snow and start it moving down the slope. As it crashes down, the avalanche picks up extra snow and can end up large enough to bury whole towns.

▲ An avalanche gathers speed as it thunders down the mountainside.

238

Marksmen shoot at snowy mountains. One way to prevent deadly avalanches is to stop too much snow from building up. In mountainous areas, marksmen set off mini avalanches on purpose. They make sure people are out of the danger zone, then fire guns to trigger a snowslide.

▼ Antarctica is a frozen wilderness. The ice piles up to form amazing shapes.

239

Ice can stay frozen for millions of years. At the North and South Poles, the weather never warms up enough for the ice to thaw. When fresh snow falls, it presses down on the snow already there, forming thick sheets. Some ice may not have melted for a million years or more.

When the wind blows

240 **Wind is moving air.** The wind blows because air is constantly moving from areas of high pressure to areas of low pressure. The bigger the difference in pressure between the two areas, the faster the wind blows.

▶ In open, exposed areas, trees can be forced into strange shapes by the wind.

241 **Winds have names.** World wind patterns are called global winds. The most famous are the trade winds that blow towards the Equator. There are also well-known local winds, such as the cold, dry mistral that blows down to southern France, or the hot, dry sirroco that blows north of the Sahara.

▼ This map shows the pattern of the world's main winds.

North Pole

Polar easterlies

Westerlies

Equator

Trade winds

Westerlies

Polar easterlies

South Pole

242 **Trade winds blow from east to west, above and below the Equator.** In the tropics, air is moving to an area of low pressure at the Equator. The winds blow towards the Equator, from the southeast in the Southern Hemisphere, and the northeast in the Northern Hemisphere. Their name comes from their importance to traders, when goods travelled across the oceans by sailing ship.

243

You can tell how windy it is by looking at the leaves on a tree. Wind strength is measured on the Beaufort Scale, named after the Irish admiral who devised it. The scale is based on the visible effects of wind, and ranges from Force 0, meaning total calm, to Force 12, which is a hurricane.

244

Wind can bring very changeable weather. The Föhn wind, which blows across Switzerland, Austria and Bavaria in southern Germany, brings with it significant and rapid rises in temperature, sometimes by as much as 30°C in a matter of hours. This has been blamed for various illnesses, including bouts of madness!

245

Wind can turn on your TV. People can harness the energy of wind to make electricity for our homes. Tall turbines are positioned in windy places. As the wind turns the turbine, the movement powers a generator and produces electrical energy.

▼ Wind energy doesn't create any harmful pollution, and it will never run out.

The Beaufort Scale

Force 0: Calm
Smoke rises straight up

Force 1: Light air
Wind motion visible in smoke

Force 2: Light breeze
Leaves rustle

Force 3: Gentle breeze
Twigs move, light flags flap

Force 4: Moderate breeze
Small branches move

Force 5: Fresh breeze
Bushes and small trees sway

Force 6: Strong breeze
Large branches in motion

Force 7: Near gale
Whole trees sway

Force 8: Gale
Difficult to walk or move, twigs break

Force 9: Strong gale
Tiles and chimneys may be blown from rooftops

Force 10: Storm
Trees uprooted

Force 11: Violent storm
Widespread damage to buildings

Force 12: Hurricane
Severe devastation

Thunderbolts and lightning

246 **Thunderstorms are most likely to occur in summer.** Hot weather creates warm, moist air that rises and forms towering cumulonimbus clouds. Inside each cloud, water droplets and ice crystals move about, building up positive and negative electrical charges. Electricity flows between the charges, creating a flash that heats the air around it. Lightning is so hot that it makes the air expand, making a loud noise, or thunderclap.

▼ Cloud-to-cloud lightning is called sheet lightning. Lightning travelling from the cloud to the ground, as shown here, is called fork lightning.

HOW CLOSE?

Lightning and thunder happen at the same time, but light travels faster than sound. Count the seconds between the flash and the clap and divide them by three. This is how many kilometres away the storm is.

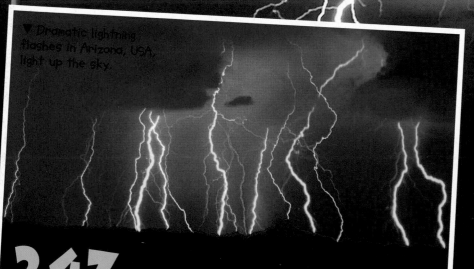

▼ Dramatic lightning flashes in Arizona, USA, light up the sky.

247 **Lightning comes in different colours.** If there is rain in the thundercloud, the lightning looks red or pink, and if there's hail, it looks blue. Lightning can also be yellow or white.

▼ Hailstones can be huge! These ones are as big as a golf ball.

248 Chunks of ice called hailstones can fall from thunderclouds. The biggest hailstones fell in Gopaljang, Bangladesh, in 1986 and weighed one kilogram each!

249 A person can survive a lightning strike. Lightning is very dangerous and can give a big enough electric shock to kill you. However, an American park ranger called Roy Sullivan survived being struck seven times.

250 Tall buildings are protected from lightning. Church steeples and other tall structures are often struck by bolts of lightning. This could damage the building, or give electric shocks to people inside, so lightning conductors are placed on the roof. These channel the lightning safely away.

◄ If lightning hits a conductor it is carried safely to the ground.

Eye of the hurricane

251 Some winds travel at speeds of more than 120 kilometres an hour. Violent tropical storms such as hurricanes happen when strong winds blow into an area of low pressure and start spinning very fast. They develop over warm seas and pick up speed until they reach land, where there is no more moist sea air to feed them.

252 The centre of a hurricane is calm and still. This part is called the 'eye'. As the eye of the storm passes over, there is a pause in the terrifying rain and wind.

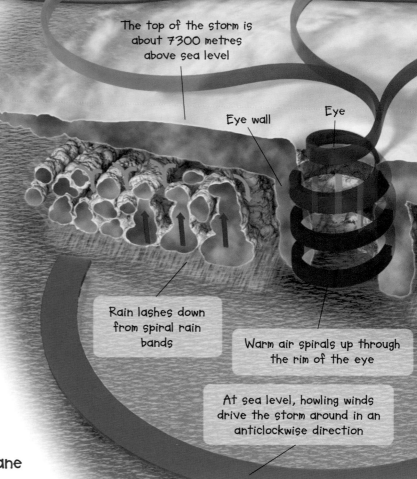

The top of the storm is about 7300 metres above sea level

Eye wall

Eye

Rain lashes down from spiral rain bands

Warm air spirals up through the rim of the eye

At sea level, howling winds drive the storm around in an anticlockwise direction

▲ This satellite photograph shows how the storm whirls around the central, still 'eye' of the hurricane.

253 Hurricane Hunters fly close to the eye of a hurricane. These are special weather planes that fly into the storm in order to take measurements such as atmospheric pressure. It is a dangerous job for the pilots, but the information they gather helps to predict the hurricane's path – and saves lives.

Top-level winds spread out air over the top of the storm in a clockwise direction

◄ The huge disc of thunderclouds that makes up a hurricane is hundreds of kilometres in diameter. The storm spins anticlockwise in the Northern Hemisphere, and clockwise in the Southern Hemisphere.

254 Hurricanes make the sea rise.
As the storm races over the ocean, its strong winds push on the seawater in front of it. This causes seawater to pile up, sometimes more than 10 metres high, which hits the shore as a storm surge. In 1961, the storm surge following Hurricane Hattie washed away Belize City in South America.

▼ Massive waves crash onto shore in Rhode Island, USA, during Superstorm Sandy in October 2012. Sandy began as a hurricane, but was downgraded to a storm.

255 Hurricanes have names.
One of the worst hurricanes was Hurricane Katrina, which battered the US coast from Florida to Texas in August 2005. The National Weather Service in the USA officially began a naming system of hurricanes in 1954, which has continued to the present day.

▼ A typhoon prevented Genghis Khan's navy from invading Japan.

256 Typhoons saved the Japanese from Genghis Khan. The 13th-century Mongol leader made two attempts to invade Japan – and both times, a terrible typhoon battered his fleet of ships and saved the Japanese!

Twisting tornadoes

257 Tornadoes spin at speeds of up to 480 kilometres an hour. These whirling columns of wind, also known as twisters, are some of Earth's most destructive storms. They form in strong thunderstorms, when the back part of the thundercloud starts spinning. The spinning air forms a funnel that reaches down towards the Earth. When it touches the ground, it becomes a tornado.

258 A tornado can be strong enough to lift a train! The spinning tornado whizzes along the ground like an enormous, high-speed vacuum cleaner, sucking up everything in its path. It rips the roofs off houses, and even tosses buildings into the air. In the 1930s, a twister in Minnesota, USA, threw a train carriage full of people over 8 metres into the air!

▶ A tornado can cause great damage to anything in its path.

I DON'T BELIEVE IT!

Loch Ness in Scotland is famous for sightings of a monster nicknamed Nessie. Perhaps people who have seen Nessie were really seeing a waterspout.

► The shaded area shows Tornado Alley, where there are hundreds of tornadoes each year.

USA

Minneapolis
Sioux Falls
Chicago
Denver
Kansas City
Wichita
St Louis
Amarillo
Oklahoma City
Dallas
Houston
New Orleans

MEXICO

259 Tornado Alley is a twister hotspot in the American Midwest. This is where hot air travelling north from the Gulf of Mexico meets cold polar winds travelling south, and creates huge thunderclouds. Of course, tornadoes can happen anywhere in the world when the conditions are right.

260 A pillar of whirling water can rise out of a lake or the sea. Waterspouts are spiralling columns of water that can be sucked up by a tornado as it forms over a lake or the sea. They tend to spin more slowly than tornadoes because water is much heavier than air.

◄ Waterspouts can suck up fish from a lake!

261 Dust devils are similar to tornadoes, and form in deserts and other dry dusty areas. They shift tonnes of sand and can cause terrible damage – stripping the paintwork from a car in seconds.

◄ A desert dust devil in Amboseli National Park, Kenya.

Sky lights

262 Rainbows are made up of seven colours. They are caused by sunlight passing through raindrops. The water acts like a glass prism, splitting the light. White light is made up of seven colours – red, orange, yellow, green, blue, indigo and violet – so these are the colours, from top to bottom, that make up the rainbow.

◄ Rainbows are often seen after rain has stopped.

263 It is not just angels that wear halos! When you look at the Sun or Moon through clouds containing tiny ice crystals, they seem to be surrounded by a glowing ring of light called a halo.

264 Two rainbows can appear at once. This is caused by the light being reflected twice inside a raindrop. The top rainbow is a reflection of the bottom one, so its colours appear the opposite way round, with the violet band at the top and red at the bottom.

265 Some rainbows appear at night. They happen when falling raindrops split moonlight, rather than sunlight. This sort of rainbow is called a moonbow. They are very rare, and can only be seen in a few places in the world.

◄ A halo around the Sun or Moon can be a sign that a storm is coming.

REMEMBER IT!

The first letter of every word of this sentence gives the first letter of each colour of the rainbow – as it appears in the sky:

Richard Of York Gave Battle In Vain

Red Orange Yellow Green Blue Indigo Violet

▼ Mock suns are also known as parhelia or sundogs.

266 **Three suns can appear in the sky.** 'Mock suns' are two bright spots that appear on either side of the Sun. They often happen at the same time as a halo, and have the same cause – light passing through ice crystals in the air.

267 **Auroras are curtains of lights in the sky.** They happen in the far north and south of the world when particles from the Sun smash into molecules in the air – at speeds of 1600 kilometres an hour. The lights may be blue, red, yellow or green.

▼ An aurora – the most dazzling natural light show on Earth!

268 **Some rainbows are just white.** Fogbows happen when sunlight passes through a patch of fog. The water droplets in the fog are too small to work like prisms, so the arching bow is white or colourless.

▼ Although a fogbow is colourless, its inner edge may appear slightly blue and its outer edge slightly red.

Animal survival

269 Camels can go for two weeks without a drink. They are adapted to life in a hot, dry climate. Camels do not sweat until their body temperature hits 40°C, which helps them to save water. Their humps are fat stores, which are used for energy when food and water is scarce.

◀ Many desert creatures, such as this gecko, come out at night when it is cooler.

270 Lizards lose salt through their noses. Most animals get rid of excess salt in their urine, but lizards, such as iguanas and geckos, live in dry parts of the world. They need to lose as little water from their bodies as possible.

◀ Being able to withstand long periods without water means that camels can survive in the harsh desert environment.

271 Even toads can survive in the desert. The spadefoot toad copes with desert conditions by staying underground in a burrow for most of the year. It only comes to the surface after a shower of rain.

◀ Beneath its gleaming–white fur, the polar bear's skin is black to absorb heat from the Sun.

272 Polar bears have black skin. These bears have all sorts of special ways to survive the polar climate. Plenty of body fat and thick fur keeps them snug and warm, while their black skin soaks up as much warmth from the Sun as possible.

QUIZ

1. What is inside a camel's hump?
2. When do spadefoot toads come out of their burrows?
3. What helps to keep polar bears warm?
4. How do lizards lose excess salt from their bodies?

Answers:
1. Fat stores 2. After rain 3. Their body fat and thick fur 4. Through their noses

273 Acorn woodpeckers store nuts for winter. Animals in temperate climates have to be prepared if they are to survive the cold winter months. Acorn woodpeckers turn tree trunks into larders. During autumn, when acorns are ripe, the birds collect as many as they can, storing them in holes that they bore into a tree.

◀ Storing acorns for food helps this woodpecker survive the cold winter months.

Myths and legends

274 People once thought the Sun was a god. The sun god was often considered to be the most important god of all, because he brought light and warmth and ripened crops. The ancient Egyptians built pyramids that pointed up to their sun god, Ra, while the Aztecs believed that their sun god, Huitzilpochtli, had even shown them where to build their capital city.

◀ The Egyptian sun god, Ra, was often shown with the head of a falcon.

275 Hurricanes are named after a god. The Mayan people lived in Central America, the part of the world that is most affected by hurricanes. Their creator god was called Huracan.

▼ Viking myths tell how Thor was killed in a great battle by a giant serpent.

276 The Vikings thought a god brought thunder. Thor was the god of war and thunder, worshipped across what is now Scandinavia. The Vikings pictured Thor as a red-bearded giant. He carried a hammer that produced bolts of lightning. Our day, Thursday, is named in Thor's honour.

277

People once danced for rain. In hot places such as Africa, people developed dances in the hope that they would bring rain. These were performed by the village shaman (a person thought to have a strong connection to spirits), using wooden instruments such as bullroarers. Sometimes water was sprinkled on the ground. Rain dances are still performed in some countries today.

278

Totem poles honoured the Thunderbird. Certain tribes of Native American Indians built tall, painted totem poles, carved in the image of the Thunderbird. They wanted to keep the spirit happy, because they thought it brought rain to feed the plants.

▶ A Native American Indian totem pole depicting the spirit of the Thunderbird.

MAKE A BULLROARER

You will need:

wooden ruler   string

Ask an adult to drill a hole in one end of the ruler. Thread through the string, and knot it, to stop it slipping through the hole. In an open space, whirl the instrument above your head to create a wind noise!

◀ A Mexican rain-dancer in traditional Mayan costume.

Weather folklore

279 'Red sky at night is the sailor's delight'. This is one of the most famous pieces of weather lore and means that a glorious sunset is followed by a fine morning. It is based on the fact that if rain clouds are in the east at sunset, meaning the rain has already passed, they light up red. The saying is also known as 'shepherd's delight'.

I DON'T BELIEVE IT!

People used to say that cows lie down when rain is coming — but there is no truth in it! They lie down whether rain is on the way or not!

▼ A beautiful sunset could help a sailor to predict the next day's weather.

280 Seaweed can tell us if rain is on the way. Long ago, people looked to nature for clues about the weather. One traditional way of forecasting was to hang up strands of seaweed. If the seaweed stayed slimy, the air was damp and rain was likely. If the seaweed shrivelled up, the weather would be dry.

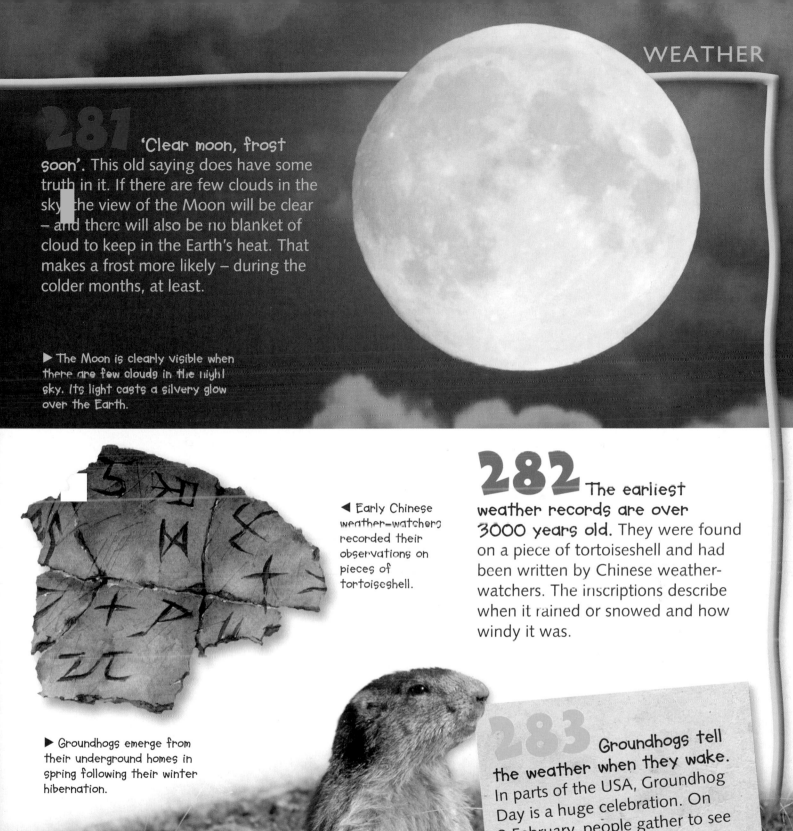

281 'Clear moon, frost soon'. This old saying does have some truth in it. If there are few clouds in the sky, the view of the Moon will be clear – and there will also be no blanket of cloud to keep in the Earth's heat. That makes a frost more likely – during the colder months, at least.

▶ The Moon is clearly visible when there are few clouds in the night sky. Its light casts a silvery glow over the Earth.

◀ Early Chinese weather-watchers recorded their observations on pieces of tortoiseshell.

282 The earliest weather records are over 3000 years old. They were found on a piece of tortoiseshell and had been written by Chinese weather-watchers. The inscriptions describe when it rained or snowed and how windy it was.

▶ Groundhogs emerge from their underground homes in spring following their winter hibernation.

283 Groundhogs tell the weather when they wake. In parts of the USA, Groundhog Day is a huge celebration. On 2 February, people gather to see the groundhog come out of its burrow. If it is cloudy and the groundhog has a shadow, it means there are six more weeks of cold to come. There is no evidence that this is true, though.

Instruments and inventors

284 The Tower of Winds was built by Andronicus of Cyrrhus in Athens, Greece around 75 BC. It is the first known weather station. It had a wind vane on the roof and a water clock inside. Its eight sides were built to face the points of the compass: north, northeast, east, southeast, south, southwest, west and northwest.

▼ This is how the Tower of Winds looks today.

285 The first barometer was made by one of Galileo's students. Barometers measure air pressure. The first person to describe and make an instrument for measuring air pressure was an Italian called Evangelista Torricelli (1608–1647). He had studied under the great scientist Galileo. Torricelli made his barometer in 1643.

◄ Torricelli took a bowl of mercury and placed it under the open end of a glass tube, also filled with mercury. It was the pressure of air on the mercury in the bowl that stopped the mercury in the tube from falling.

286 Weather vanes have been used since around 50 BC. They are placed on the highest point of a building, and have four fixed pointers to show north, south, east and west. A shape on the top swivels freely, so when the wind blows it points in the direction that the wind is blowing from.

287 **A weather house really can predict the weather.** It is a type of hygrometer – an instrument that detects how much moisture is in the air. If there is lots, the rainy-day character comes out of the door!

◀ Weather houses have two figures. One comes out when the air is damp, and the other when the air is dry.

◀ Ships, cockerels and many other shapes are used to indicate wind direction on weather vanes.

288 **Fahrenheit made the first thermometer in 1714.** Thermometers are instruments that measure temperature. Gabriel Daniel Fahrenheit (1686–1736) invented the thermometer using a blob of mercury sealed in an airtight tube. The Fahrenheit scale for measuring heat was named after him. The Centigrade scale was introduced in 1742 by the Swedish scientist Anders Celsius (1701–1744).

▶ Anders Celsius came from a family of scientists and astronomers.

▲ This early thermometer shows both the Fahrenheit and the Celsius temperature scales.

What's the forecast?

289 Predicting the weather is called forecasting. Forecasters study the atmosphere and look at past weather patterns. They then use supercomputers to work out what the weather will be like over the next few days. But sometimes even forecasters get it wrong!

 A cold front is shown by a blue triangle

 A warm front is shown by a red semi-circle

 Black lines with red semi-circles and blue triangles show where a cold front meets a warm front

 White lines called isobars connect places of equal air pressure

 This symbol shows wind strength and direction. The circle shows how much cloud cover there is

 This symbol shows that the wind is very strong — look at the three lines on the tail

This shows an area of calm, with some cloud cover

▲ Meteorologists call their weather maps synoptic charts. The symbols they use make up a common language for weather scientists all around the world.

▲ Meteorologists (weather scientists) use modern technology to accurately track and predict the weather.

290 Nations need to share weather data. By 1865, nearly 60 weather stations across Europe were swapping information. These early weather scientists, or meteorologists, realized that they needed to present their data using symbols that they could all understand. Today, meteorologists still plot their data on maps called synoptic charts. Lines called isobars link areas of the same air pressure and other symbols indicate temperature and wind.

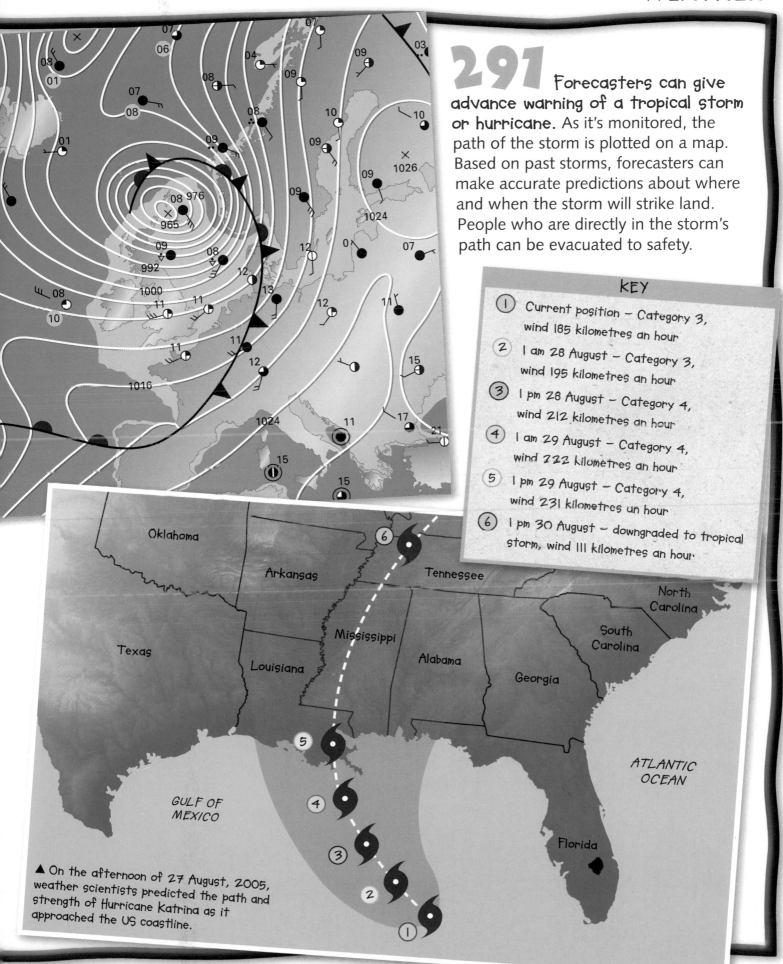

291 Forecasters can give advance warning of a tropical storm or hurricane. As it's monitored, the path of the storm is plotted on a map. Based on past storms, forecasters can make accurate predictions about where and when the storm will strike land. People who are directly in the storm's path can be evacuated to safety.

KEY

① Current position – Category 3, wind 185 kilometres an hour

② 1 am 28 August – Category 3, wind 195 kilometres an hour

③ 1 pm 28 August – Category 4, wind 212 kilometres an hour

④ 1 am 29 August – Category 4, wind 222 kilometres an hour

⑤ 1 pm 29 August – Category 4, wind 231 kilometres an hour

⑥ 1 pm 30 August – downgraded to tropical storm, wind 111 kilometres an hour

▲ On the afternoon of 27 August, 2005, weather scientists predicted the path and strength of Hurricane Katrina as it approached the US coastline.

Weather watch

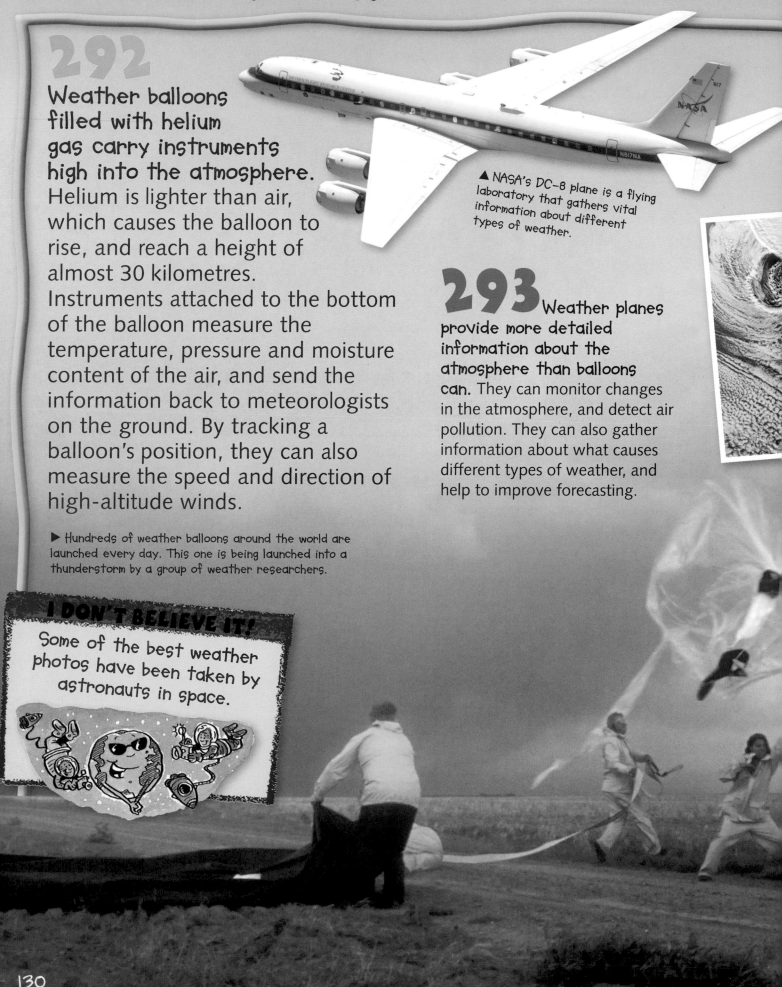

292 Weather balloons filled with helium gas carry instruments high into the atmosphere. Helium is lighter than air, which causes the balloon to rise, and reach a height of almost 30 kilometres. Instruments attached to the bottom of the balloon measure the temperature, pressure and moisture content of the air, and send the information back to meteorologists on the ground. By tracking a balloon's position, they can also measure the speed and direction of high-altitude winds.

▶ Hundreds of weather balloons around the world are launched every day. This one is being launched into a thunderstorm by a group of weather researchers.

▲ NASA's DC-8 plane is a flying laboratory that gathers vital information about different types of weather.

293 Weather planes provide more detailed information about the atmosphere than balloons can. They can monitor changes in the atmosphere, and detect air pollution. They can also gather information about what causes different types of weather, and help to improve forecasting.

I DON'T BELIEVE IT!

Some of the best weather photos have been taken by astronauts in space.

294 Weather satellites can provide a wide range of vital information. From such a long way above the Earth, their cameras can spot the distinctive spiralling cloud pattern of a tropical storm while it is still mid-ocean. This helps forecasters to issue warnings in good time. Satellites are also equipped with heat-sensitive infra-red cameras, which measure cloud temperature – important in forecasting snowfall. Satellite-based radar can also measure the thickness of any cloud cover, and the height of waves at sea.

▲ A weather satellite takes photographs of Earth's weather systems from space.

▲ A satellite photograph showing two spiral weather systems in the North Atlantic Ocean.

295 Ground-based weather radar that can detect rainfall and wind speed is used at airports. Knowledge of the exact weather conditions is critical for pilots during take-off and landing. Weather radar is also used to track the formation and path of tornadoes, and at sea, radar can give warning of icebergs.

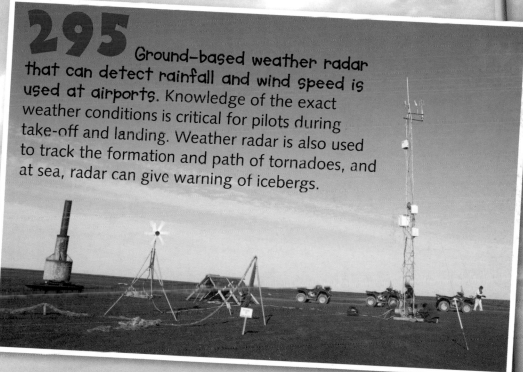

▶ Weather information is collected from even the remotest parts of the globe. This weather monitoring station is inside the Arctic Circle.

Changing climate

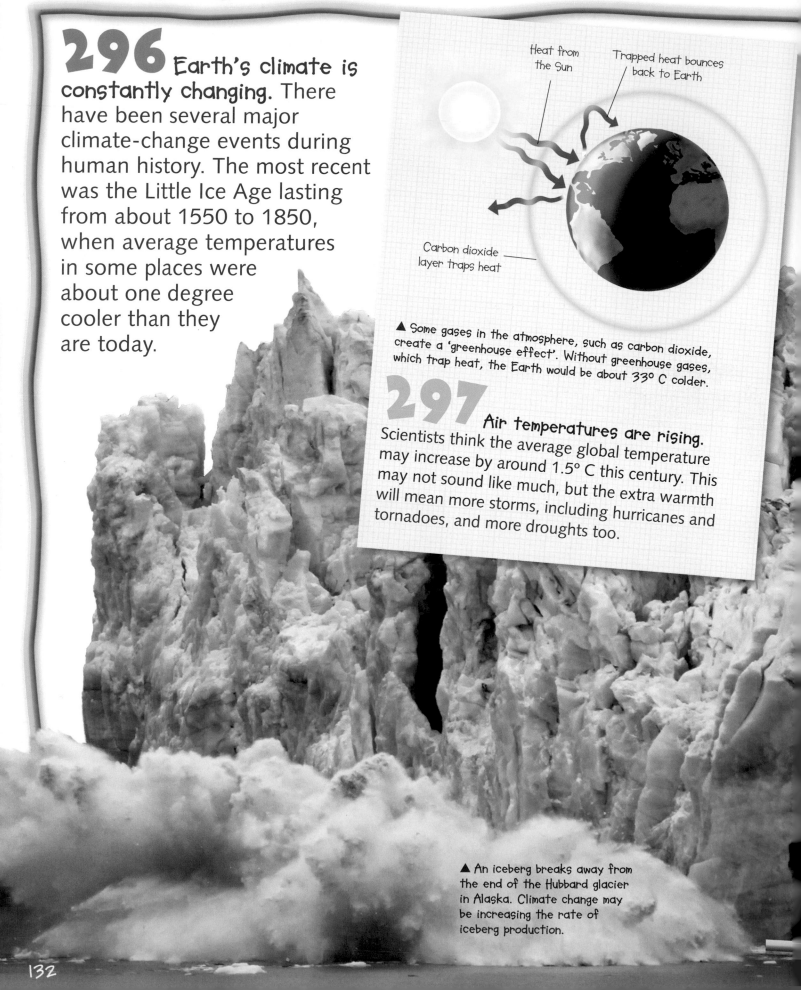

296 Earth's climate is constantly changing. There have been several major climate-change events during human history. The most recent was the Little Ice Age lasting from about 1550 to 1850, when average temperatures in some places were about one degree cooler than they are today.

Heat from the Sun

Trapped heat bounces back to Earth

Carbon dioxide layer traps heat

▲ Some gases in the atmosphere, such as carbon dioxide, create a 'greenhouse effect'. Without greenhouse gases, which trap heat, the Earth would be about 33° C colder.

297 Air temperatures are rising. Scientists think the average global temperature may increase by around 1.5° C this century. This may not sound like much, but the extra warmth will mean more storms, including hurricanes and tornadoes, and more droughts too.

▲ An iceberg breaks away from the end of the Hubbard glacier in Alaska. Climate change may be increasing the rate of iceberg production.

298
Tree–felling is affecting our weather. In areas of Southeast Asia and South America, rainforests are being cleared for farming. When the trees are burned, the fires release carbon dioxide – a greenhouse gas that helps to blanket the Earth and keep in the heat. High levels of carbon dioxide raise the temperature too much.

▶ Like all plants, rainforest trees take in carbon dioxide and give out oxygen. As rainforests are destroyed, the amount of carbon dioxide in the atmosphere increases.

299
Some sea creatures, such as the colourful corals that live mainly in shallow water, are very sensitive to temperature. As the atmosphere gradually warms up, so does the temperature of the surface water. This causes the coral animals, called polyps, to die, leaving behind their lifeless, stony skeletons.

◀ The death of corals through changes in water temperature is known as 'bleaching'.

300
The long-term effects of climate change are uncertain. In the short-term it seems very likely that the climate will become more unstable, and that there will be an increase in the number and intensity of extreme weather events. Weather forecasting has always been important, but in the future it will become even more so as we adapt to Earth's changing climate.

HUMAN BODY

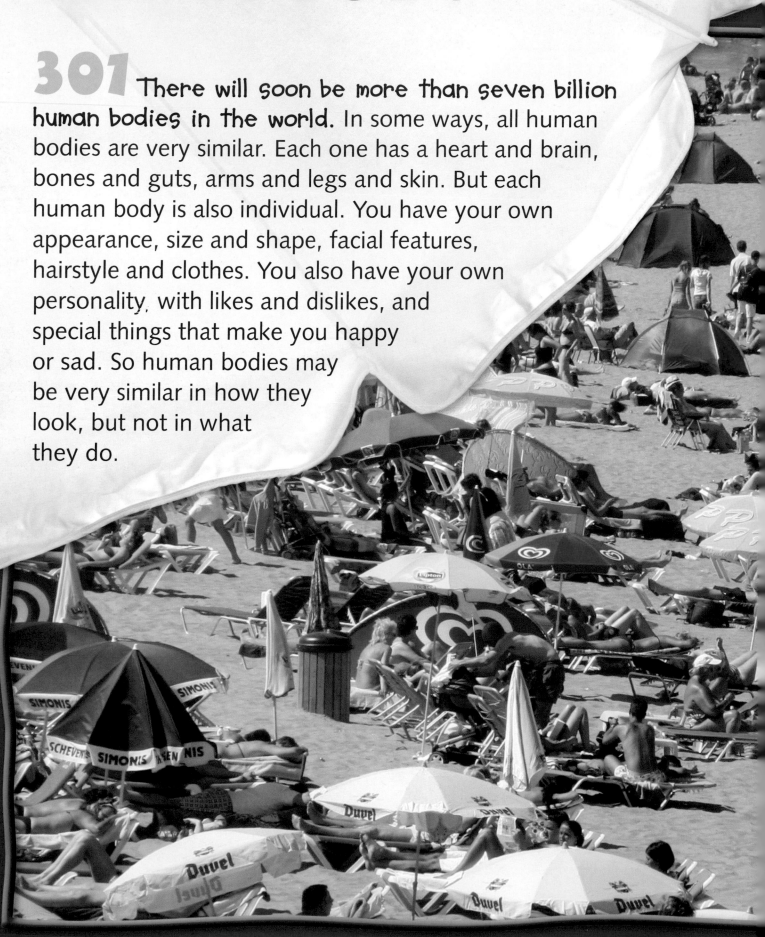

301 **There will soon be more than seven billion human bodies in the world.** In some ways, all human bodies are very similar. Each one has a heart and brain, bones and guts, arms and legs and skin. But each human body is also individual. You have your own appearance, size and shape, facial features, hairstyle and clothes. You also have your own personality, with likes and dislikes, and special things that make you happy or sad. So human bodies may be very similar in how they look, but not in what they do.

▲ We tend to notice small differences on the outside of human bodies, such as height, width, hair colour and clothes. This allows us to recognize our family and friends.

Baby body

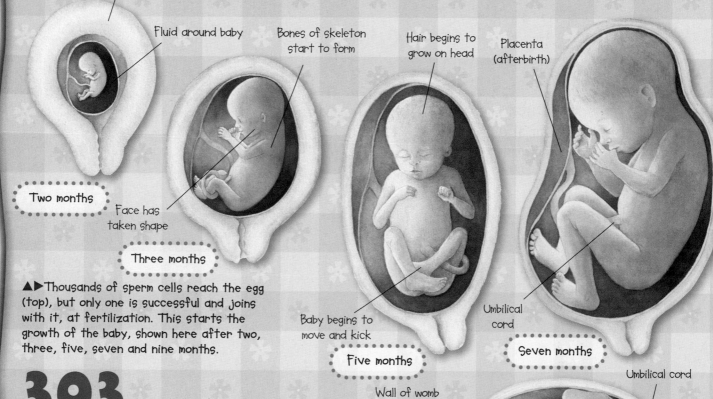

Successful sperm

Egg cell

302 A full-grown human body is made of billions of microscopic parts, called cells. But in the beginning, the body is a single cell, smaller than this full stop. Yet it contains all the instructions, known as genes, for the whole body to grow and develop.

Wall of uterus

Fluid around baby

Bones of skeleton start to form

Hair begins to grow on head

Placenta (afterbirth)

Two months

Face has taken shape

Three months

▲▶Thousands of sperm cells reach the egg (top), but only one is successful and joins with it, at fertilization. This starts the growth of the baby, shown here after two, three, five, seven and nine months.

Baby begins to move and kick

Umbilical cord

Five months

Seven months

Umbilical cord

303 The body begins when an egg cell inside the mother joins up with sperm from the father. The egg cell splits into two cells, then into four cells, then eight, and so on. The bundle of cells embeds itself in the mother's womb (uterus), which protects and nourishes it. Soon there are thousands of cells, then millions, forming a tiny embryo. After two months the embryo has grown into a tiny baby, as big as your thumb, with arms, legs, eyes, ears and a mouth.

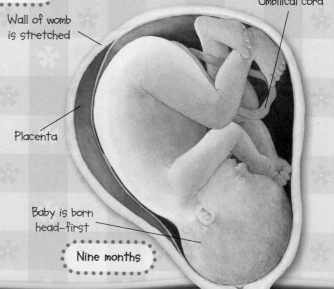

Wall of womb is stretched

Placenta

Baby is born head-first

Nine months

Cervix (neck of womb)

304 After nine months in the womb, the baby is ready to be born. Strong muscles in the walls of the womb tighten, or contract. They push the baby through the opening, or neck of the womb, called the cervix, and along the birth canal. The baby enters the outside world.

305 A newborn baby may be frightened and usually starts to cry. Inside the womb it was warm, wet, dark, quiet and cramped. Outside there are lights, noises, voices, fresh air and room to stretch. The crying is also helpful to start the baby breathing, using its own lungs.

306 Being born can take an hour or two — or a whole day or two. It is very tiring for both the baby and its mother. After birth, the baby starts to feel hungry and it feeds on its mother's milk. Finally, mother and baby settle down for a rest and some sleep.

I DON'T BELIEVE IT!

The human body never grows as fast again as it does during the first weeks in the womb. If the body kept growing at that rate, every day for 50 years, it would be bigger than the biggest mountain in the world!

▲ Once the baby is settled it is time for its mother to admire her newborn and rest.

The growing body

307
A new baby just seems to eat, sleep and cry. It feeds on milk when hungry and sleeps when tired. Also, it cries when it is too hot, too cold, or when its nappy needs changing.

308
A new baby is not totally helpless. It can do simple actions called reflexes, to help it survive. If something touches the baby's cheek, it turns its head to that side and tries to suck. If the baby hears a loud noise, it opens its eyes wide, throws out its arms and cries for help. If something touches the baby's hand and fingers, it grasps tightly.

309
A new baby looks, listens, touches and quickly learns. Gradually it starts to recognize voices, faces and places. After about six weeks, it begins to smile. Inside the body, the baby's brain is learning very quickly. The baby soon knows that if it laughs, people will laugh back and if it cries, someone will come to look after it.

QUIZ

Most babies learn to do certain actions in the same order. The order is mixed up here. Can you put it right?

walk, crawl, roll over, sit up, smile, stand

Answer:
smile, roll over, sit up,
crawl, stand, walk

▼ In the grasping reflex, the baby tightly holds anything that touches its hand or fingers. Its grip is surprisingly strong!

▼ Most babies crawl before they walk, but some go straight from sitting or 'bottom-shuffling' to walking.

311
As a baby grows into a child, at around 18 months, it learns ten new words every day, from 'cat' and 'dog' to 'sun' and 'moon'. There are new games such as piling up bricks, new actions such as throwing and kicking, and new skills such as using a spoon at mealtimes and scribbling on paper.

310
At about three months old, most babies can reach out to hold something, and roll over when lying down. By the age of six months, most babies can sit up and hold food in their fingers. At nine months, many babies are crawling well and perhaps standing up. By their first birthday, many babies are learning to walk and starting to talk.

312
At the age of five, when most children start school, they continue to learn an amazing amount. This includes thinking or mental skills such as counting and reading, and precise movements such as writing and drawing. They learn out of the classroom too – how to play with friends and share.

▶ Playing is lots of fun, but it's learning too, as children develop control over the muscles in their fast-growing bodies.

On the body's outside

313 Skin's surface is made of tiny cells that have filled up with a hard, tough substance called keratin, and then died. So when you look at a human body, most of what you see is 'dead'! The cells get rubbed off as you move, have a wash and get dry.

314 Skin rubs off all the time, and grows all the time too. Just under the surface, living cells make more new cells that gradually fill with keratin, die and move up to the surface. It takes about four weeks from a new skin cell being made to when it reaches the surface and is rubbed off. This upper layer of skin is called the epidermis.

Hair

Oil gland

Epidermis

Dermis

Hair follicle

▲ This view shows skin magnified (enlarged) about 50 times.

▲ Lots of dead skin is removed without you realizing when you dry yourself after a shower.

315 Skin's lower layer, the dermis, is thicker than the epidermis. It is made of tiny, bendy, thread-like fibres of the substance collagen. The dermis also contains small blood vessels, tiny sweat glands, and micro-sensors that detect touch.

316
One of skin's important jobs is to protect the body. It stops the delicate inner parts from being rubbed, knocked or scraped. Skin also prevents body fluids from leaking away and it keeps out dirt and germs.

317
Skin helps to keep the body at the same temperature. If you become too hot, sweat oozes onto your skin and, as it dries, draws heat from the body. Also, the blood vessels in the lower layer of skin widen, to lose more heat through the skin. This is why a hot person looks sweaty and red in the face.

318
Skin gives us our sense of touch. Millions of microscopic sensors in the lower layer of skin, the dermis, are joined by nerves to the brain. These sensors detect different kinds of touch, from a light stroke to heavy pressure, heat or cold, and movement. Pain sensors detect when skin is damaged. Ouch!

Safety helmet protects head and brain

Elbow-pads cushion fall

Gloves save fingers from scrapes and breaks

Knee-pads prevent hard bumps

▲ Skin is tough, but it sometimes needs help to protect the body. Otherwise it, and the body parts beneath, may get damaged.

SENSITIVE SKIN

You will need:
a friend   sticky-tack
two used matchsticks   ruler

1. Press some sticky-tack on the end of the ruler. Press two matchsticks into the sticky-tack, standing upright, about 1 centimetre apart.

2. Make your friend look away. Touch the back of their hand with both matchstick ends. Ask your friend: 'Is that one matchstick or two?' Sensitive skin can detect both ends

3. Try this at several places, such as on the finger, wrist, forearm, neck and cheek.

Hair and nails

319 There are about 120,000 hairs on the head, called scalp hairs. There are also eyebrow hairs and eyelash hairs. Grown-ups have hairs in the armpits and between the legs, and men have hairs on the face. And everyone, even a baby, has tiny hairs all over the body – 5 to 10 million of them!

Blonde wavy hair is the result of carotene from an oval hair follicle

Black curly hair is the result of black melanin from a flat hair follicle

Straight red hair is the result of red melanin from a round hair follicle

◄ Hair contains pigments (coloured substances) – mainly melanin (dark brown) and some carotene (yellowish). Different amounts of pigments, and the way their tiny particles are spread out, cause different hair colours.

320 Each hair grows from a deep pit in the skin, called a follicle. The hair is only alive where it gets longer, at its base or root, in the bottom of the follicle. The rest of the hair, called the shaft, is like the surface of the skin – hard, tough, dead and made of keratin. Hair helps to protect the body, especially where it is thicker and longer on the head. It also helps to keep the body warm in cold conditions.

Straight black hair is the result of black melanin from a round follicle

321 Scalp hairs get longer by about 3 millimetres each week, on average. Eyebrow hairs grow more slowly. No hairs live forever. Each one grows for a time, then it falls out, and its follicle has a 'rest' before a new hair sprouts. This is happening all the time, so the body always has some hairs on each part.

322 Nails, like hairs, grow at their base (the nail root) and are made of keratin. Also like hairs, nails grow faster in summer than in winter, and faster at night than by day. Nails lengthen by about half a millimetre, on average, each week.

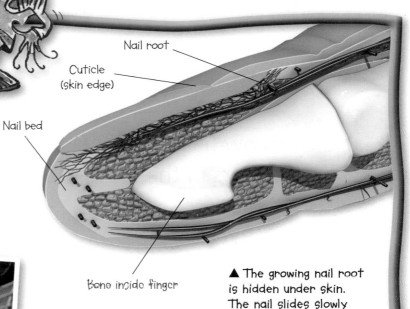

Nail root
Cuticle (skin edge)
Nail bed
Bone inside finger

▲ The growing nail root is hidden under skin. The nail slides slowly along the nail bed.

▲ Nails make the fingertips stronger and more rigid for pressing hard on guitar strings. Slightly longer nails pluck the strings.

323 Nails have many uses, from peeling off sticky labels to plucking guitar strings or scratching an itch. They protect and stiffen the ends of the fingers, where there are nerves that give us our sense of touch.

I DON'T BELIEVE IT!

A scalp hair grows for up to five years before it falls out and gets replaced. Left uncut during this time, it would be about one metre long. But some people have unusual hair that grows faster and for longer. Each hair can reach more than 5 metres in length before dropping out.

▶ Keeping your nails clean is very important. If you don't, germs can build up under your nails and make you ill.

The bony body

324 Without bones, the body would be as floppy as a jellyfish! Bones do many jobs. The long bones in the arms work like levers to reach out the hands. The finger bones grasp and grip. Bones protect softer body parts. The dome-like skull protects the brain. The ribs shield the lungs and heart. Bones also produce blood cells, as explained on the opposite page.

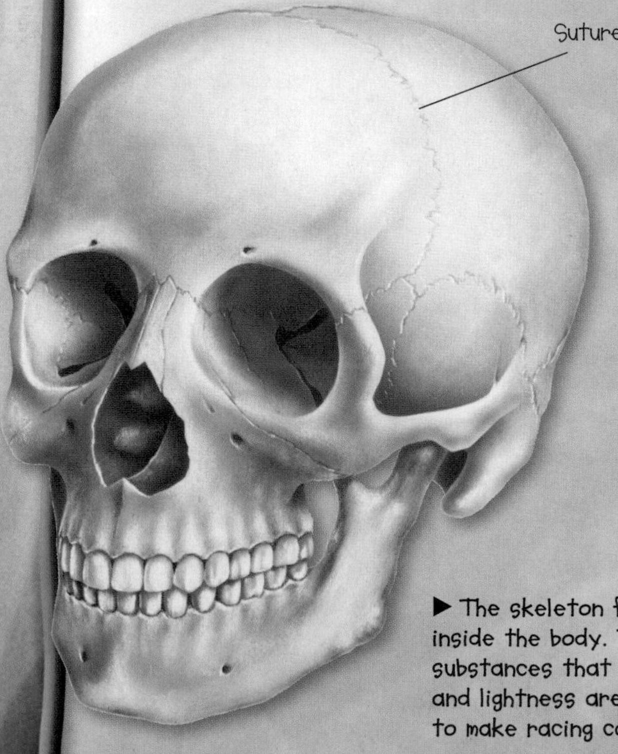

Cranium (skull)

Mandible (lower jaw)

Sternum (breastbone)

Clavicle (collarbone)

Rib

Humerus

Vertebra (backbone)

Ulna

Radius

Pelvis (hip bone)

Suture

◀ The skull has deep bowls for the eyes, and small holes where nerves pass through to join the brain inside.

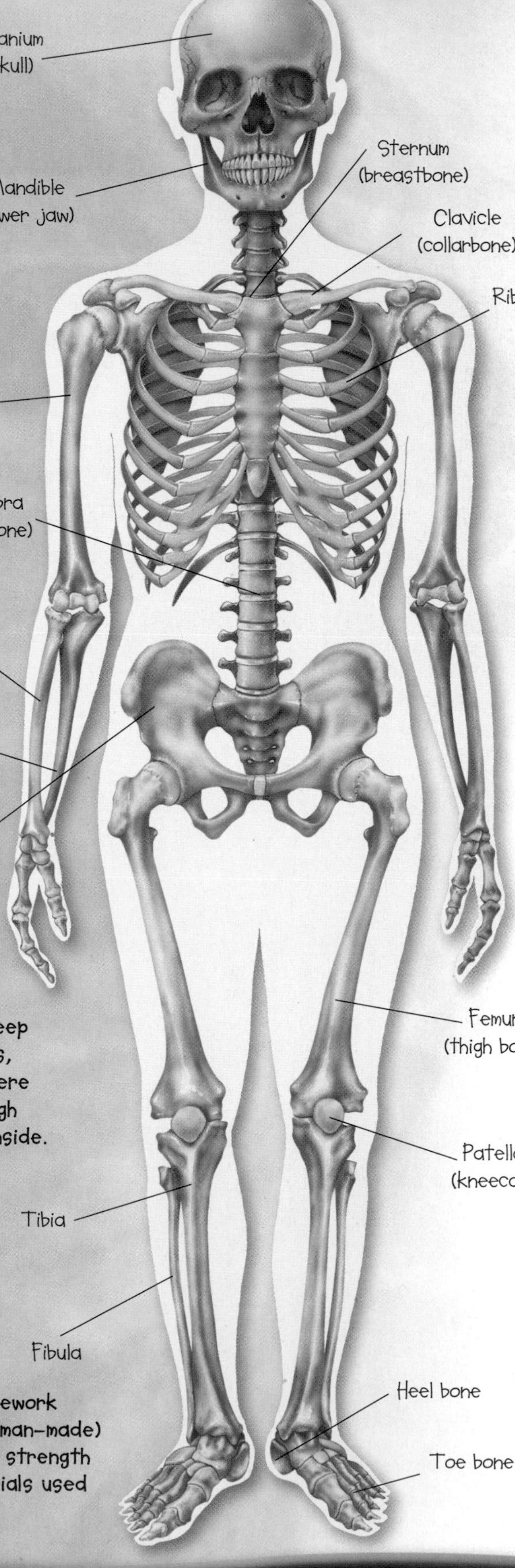

Femur (thigh bone)

Patella (kneecap)

Tibia

Fibula

Heel bone

Toe bone

▶ The skeleton forms a strong framework inside the body. The only artificial (man-made) substances that can match bone for strength and lightness are some of the materials used to make racing cars and jet planes.

325

All the bones together make up the skeleton. Most people have 206 bones, from head to toe as follows:

- 8 in the upper part of the skull, the cranium or braincase
- 14 in the face
- 6 tiny ear bones, 3 deep in each ear
- 1 in the neck, which is floating and not directly connected to any other bone
- 26 in the spinal column or backbone
- 25 in the chest, being 24 ribs and the breastbone
- 32 in each arm, from shoulder to fingertips (8 in each wrist)
- 31 in each leg, from hip to toetips (7 in each ankle)

326

Bone contains threads of the tough, slightly bendy substance called collagen. It also has hard minerals such as calcium and phosphate. Together, the collagen and minerals make a bone strong and rigid, yet able to bend slightly under stress. Bones have blood vessels for nourishment and nerves to feel pressure and pain. Also, some bones are not solid. They contain a jelly-like substance called marrow. This makes tiny parts for the blood, called red and white blood cells.

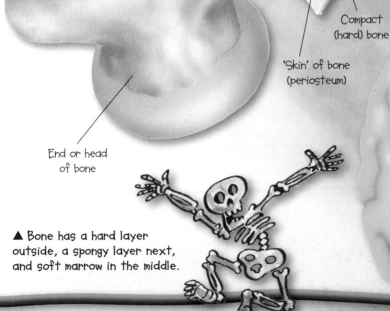

Spongy bone

Marrow

Nerves and blood vessels

Compact (hard) bone

'Skin' of bone (periosteum)

End or head of bone

▲ Bone has a hard layer outside, a spongy layer next, and soft marrow in the middle.

QUIZ

Every bone has a scientific or medical name, and many have ordinary names too. Can you match up these ordinary and scientific names for various bones?

1. Mandible 2. Femur 3. Clavicle
4. Pelvis 5. Patella 6. Sternum

a. Thigh bone b. Breastbone
c. Kneecap d. Hip bone
e. Collarbone f. Lower jaw bone

Answers:
1f 2a 3e 4d 5c 6b

The flexible body

327 Without joints, almost the only parts of your body that could move would be your tongue and eyebrows! Joints between bones allow the skeleton to bend. You have more than 200 joints. The largest are in the hips and knees. The smallest are in the fingers, toes, and between the tiny bones inside each ear which help you hear.

328 There are several kinds of joints, depending on the shapes of the bone ends, and how much the bones can move. Bend your knee and your lower leg moves forwards and backwards, but not sideways. This is a hinge-type joint. Bend your hip and your leg can move forwards, backwards, and also from side to side. This is a ball-and-socket joint.

► This X-ray shows a dislocated (out of place) shoulder. The shoulder joint has the biggest range of movement, so this injury is common.

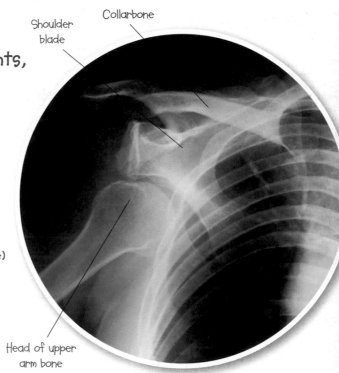

Shoulder blade

Collarbone

Head of upper arm bone

QUIZ

Try using these different joints carefully, and see how much movement they allow. Can you guess the type of joint used in each one – hinge or ball-and-socket?

1. Fingertip joint (smallest knuckle)
2. Elbow
3. Hip
4. Shoulder

Answers:
1. hinge 2. hinge
3. ball-and-socket 4. ball-and-socket

329 Inside a joint where the bones come together, each bone end is covered with a smooth, shiny, slippery, slightly springy substance, known as cartilage. This is smeared with a thick liquid called synovial fluid. The fluid works like the oil in a car, to smooth the movements and reduce rubbing and wear between the cartilage surfaces.

146

330

The bones in a joint are linked together by a bag-like part, the capsule, and strong, stretchy, strap-like ligaments. The ligaments let the bones move but stop them coming apart or moving too far. The shoulder has seven strong ligaments.

331

In some joints, there are cartilage coverings over the bone ends and also pads of cartilage between the cartilage! These extra pads are called articular discs. There is one in each joint in the backbone, between the spinal bones, which are called vertebrae. There are also two of these extra cartilages, known as menisci, in each knee joint. They help the knee to 'lock' straight so that we can stand up without too much effort.

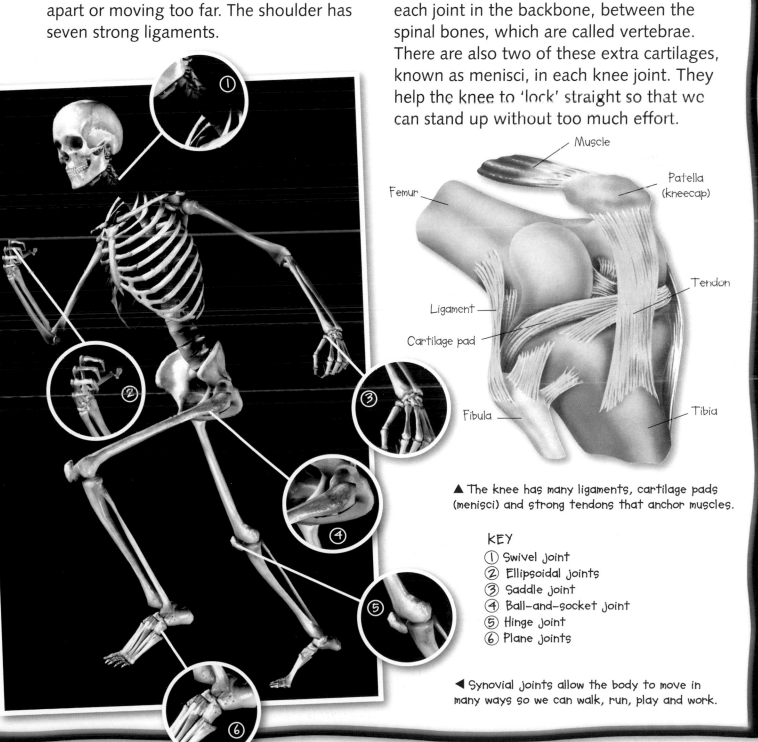

Muscle

Femur

Patella (kneecap)

Tendon

Ligament

Cartilage pad

Fibula

Tibia

▲ The knee has many ligaments, cartilage pads (menisci) and strong tendons that anchor muscles.

KEY
① Swivel joint
② Ellipsoidal joints
③ Saddle joint
④ Ball-and-socket joint
⑤ Hinge joint
⑥ Plane joints

◄ Synovial joints allow the body to move in many ways so we can walk, run, play and work.

When muscles pull

332 Almost half the body's weight is muscles, and there are more than 640 of them! Muscles have one simple but important job, which is to get shorter, or contract. A muscle cannot forcefully get longer.

▼ A tendon is stuck firmly into the bone it pulls, with a joint stronger than superglue!

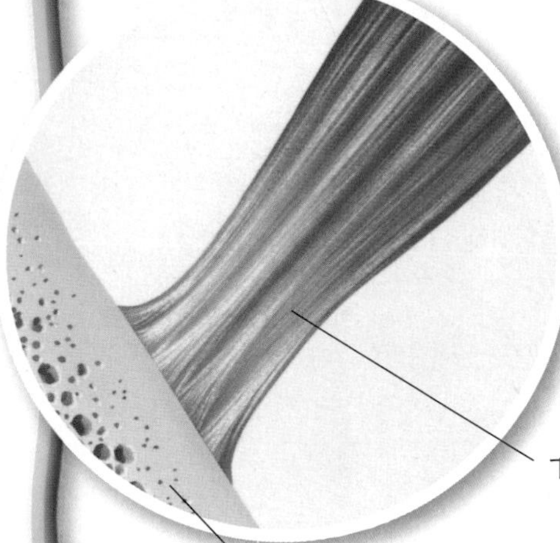

Tendon

Bone

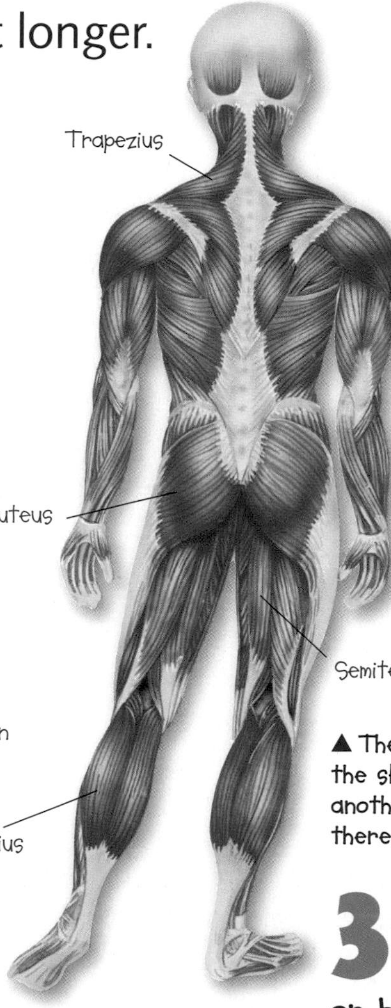

Pectoralis

Biceps

Deltoid

Abdominal wall muscles

Trapezius

Rectus femoris

Gluteus

Semitendinosus

Gastrocnemius

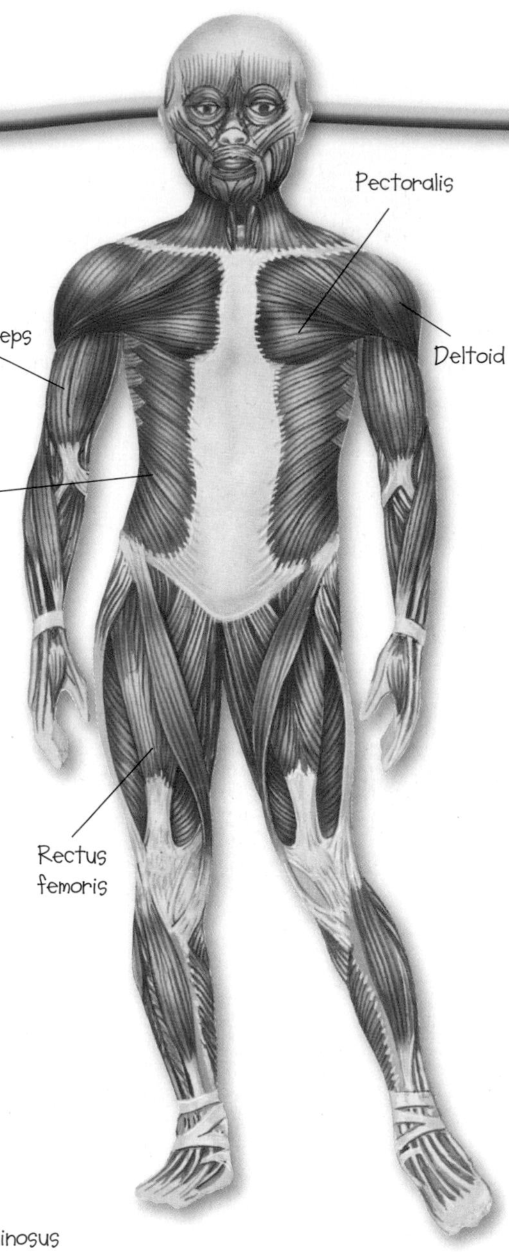

▲ The muscles shown here are those just beneath the skin, called superficial muscles. Under them is another layer, the deep muscle layer. In some areas there is an additional layer, the medial muscles.

333 A muscle is joined to a bone by its tendon. This is where the end of the muscle becomes slimmer or tapers, and is strengthened by strong, thick fibres of collagen. The fibres are fixed firmly into the surface of the bone.

334 Some muscles are wide or broad, and shaped more like flat sheets or triangles. These include the three layers of muscles in the lower front and sides of the body, called the abdominal wall muscles. If you tense or contract them, they pull your tummy in to make you look thinner.

335 Most muscles are long and slim, and joined to bones at each end. As they contract they pull on the bones and move them. As this happens, the muscle becomes wider, or more bulging in the middle. To move the bone back again, a muscle on the other side of it contracts, while the first muscle relaxes and is pulled longer.

I DON'T BELIEVE IT!

It's easier to smile than to frown. There are about 40 muscles under the skin of the face. You use almost all of these to make a deep frown, but only about half of them to show a broad grin.

336 Every muscle in the body has a scientific or medical name, which is often quite long and complicated. Some of these names are familiar to people who do exercise and sports. The 'pecs' are the pectoralis major muscles across the chest. The 'biceps' are the biceps brachii muscles in the upper arms, which bulge when you bend your elbow.

337 If you take plenty of exercise or play sport, you do not gain new muscles. But the muscles you have become larger and stronger. This keeps them fit and healthy. Muscles which are not used much may become weak and floppy.

▶ A breakdancer needs endurance, strength and control over their muscles to carry out moves such as this.

Biceps gets shorter and bends the elbow

To move the forearm back down, the triceps shortens and the biceps gets longer

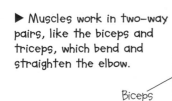

▶ Muscles work in two-way pairs, like the biceps and triceps, which bend and straighten the elbow.

Biceps

Triceps

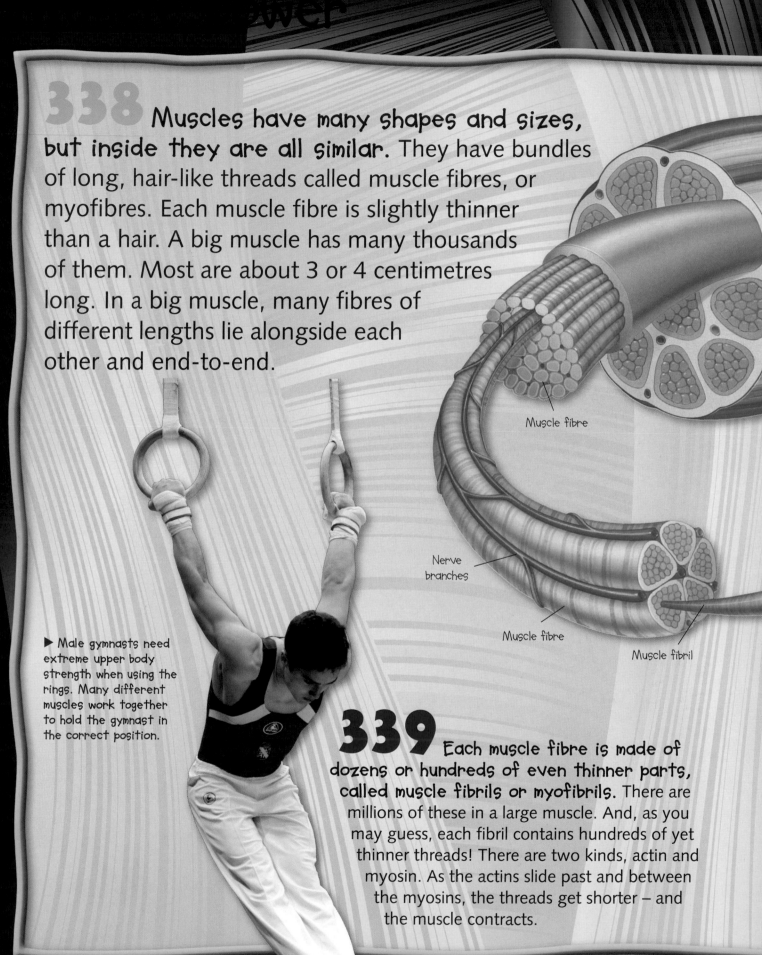

338 **Muscles have many shapes and sizes, but inside they are all similar.** They have bundles of long, hair-like threads called muscle fibres, or myofibres. Each muscle fibre is slightly thinner than a hair. A big muscle has many thousands of them. Most are about 3 or 4 centimetres long. In a big muscle, many fibres of different lengths lie alongside each other and end-to-end.

Muscle fibre

Nerve branches

Muscle fibre

Muscle fibril

▶ Male gymnasts need extreme upper body strength when using the rings. Many different muscles work together to hold the gymnast in the correct position.

339 Each muscle fibre is made of dozens or hundreds of even thinner parts, called muscle fibrils or myofibrils. There are millions of these in a large muscle. And, as you may guess, each fibril contains hundreds of yet thinner threads! There are two kinds, actin and myosin. As the actins slide past and between the myosins, the threads get shorter – and the muscle contracts.

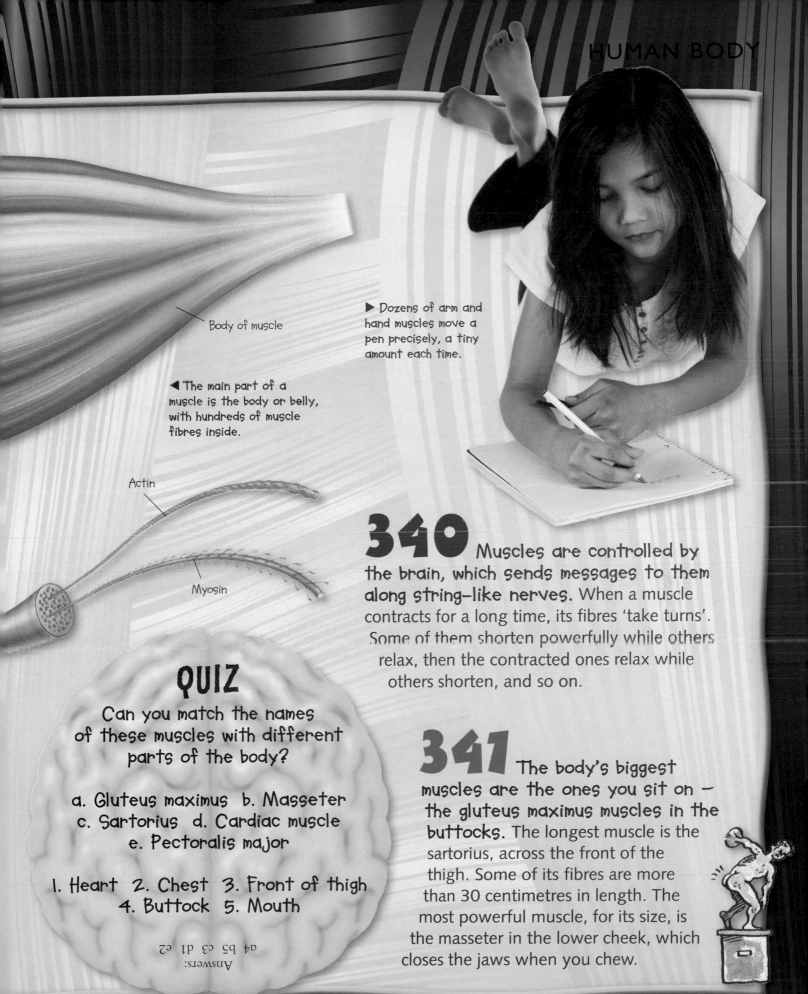

Body of muscle

► Dozens of arm and hand muscles move a pen precisely, a tiny amount each time.

◄ The main part of a muscle is the body or belly, with hundreds of muscle fibres inside.

Actin

Myosin

340 Muscles are controlled by the brain, which sends messages to them along string-like nerves. When a muscle contracts for a long time, its fibres 'take turns'. Some of them shorten powerfully while others relax, then the contracted ones relax while others shorten, and so on.

QUIZ

Can you match the names of these muscles with different parts of the body?

a. Gluteus maximus b. Masseter
c. Sartorius d. Cardiac muscle
e. Pectoralis major

1. Heart 2. Chest 3. Front of thigh
4. Buttock 5. Mouth

Answers:
a4 b5 c3 d1 e2

341 The body's biggest muscles are the ones you sit on – the gluteus maximus muscles in the buttocks. The longest muscle is the sartorius, across the front of the thigh. Some of its fibres are more than 30 centimetres in length. The most powerful muscle, for its size, is the masseter in the lower cheek, which closes the jaws when you chew.

The breathing body

342 The body cannot survive more than a few minutes without breathing. This action is so important, we do it all the time without thinking. We breathe to take air into the body. Air contains the gas oxygen, which is needed to get energy from food to power all of the body's vital life processes.

▶ Body parts make up the respiratory system in the head, neck and chest. These carry out the process of breathing air to take oxygen into the body.

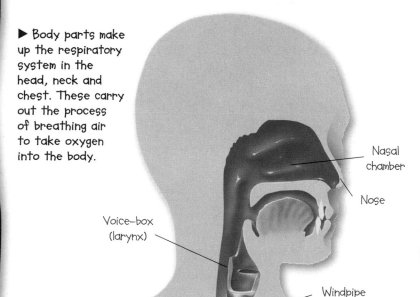

Nasal chamber

Nose

Voice-box (larynx)

Windpipe

Bronchus

Left lung

Diaphragm

▲ Scuba divers wear special breathing apparatus called 'aqua lungs'. They control their breathing to make their oxygen supply last as long as possible.

343 Parts of the body that work together to carry out a main task are called a system — so the parts that carry out breathing are the respiratory system. These parts are the nose, throat, windpipe, the air tubes or bronchi in the chest, and the lungs.

344

The nose is the entrance for fresh air to the lungs – and the exit for stale air from the lungs. The soft, moist lining inside the nose makes air warmer and damper, which is better for the lungs. Tiny bits of floating dust and germs stick to the lining or the hairs in the nose, making the air cleaner.

▼ When playing the trumpet, the diaphragm and chest control the air flowing in and out of the lungs.

345

The windpipe, or trachea, is a tube leading from the back of the nose and mouth, down to the lungs. It has about 20 C-shaped hoops of cartilage in its wall to keep it open, like a vacuum cleaner hose. Otherwise the pressure of body parts in the neck and chest would squash it shut.

346

At the top of the windpipe, making a bulge at the front of the neck, is the voice-box or larynx. It has two stiff flaps, vocal cords, which stick out from its sides. Normally these flaps are apart for easy breathing. But muscles in the voice-box can pull the flaps almost together. As air passes through the narrow slit between them it makes the flaps shake or vibrate – and this is the sound of your voice.

HUMMMMMM!

You will need:
stopwatch

Do you think making sounds with your voice-box uses more air than breathing? Find out by following this experiment.

1. Take a deep breath in, then breathe out at your normal rate, for as long as you can. Time the out-breath.

2. Take a similar deep breath in, then hum as you breathe out, again for as long as you can. Time the hum.

3. Try the same while whispering your favourite song, then again when singing.

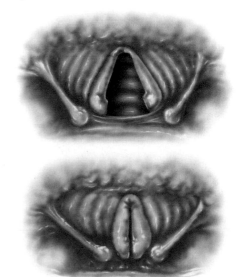

▲ The vocal cords are held apart for breathing (top) and pulled together for speech (bottom).

Breathing bits

347 The main parts of the respiratory (breathing) system are the two lungs in the chest. Each one is shaped like a tall cone, with the pointed end at shoulder level.

348 Air comes in and out of the lungs along the windpipe, which branches at its base to form two main air tubes, the bronchi. One goes to each lung. Inside the lung, each bronchus divides again and again, becoming narrower each time. Finally the air tubes, thinner than hairs, end at groups of tiny 'bubbles' called alveoli.

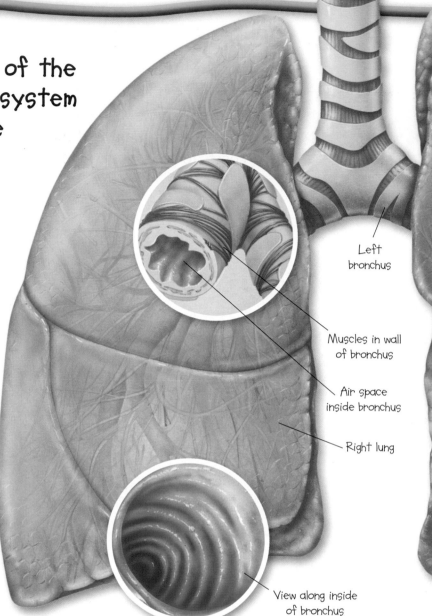

Left bronchus

Muscles in wall of bronchus

Air space inside bronchus

Right lung

View along inside of bronchus

I DON'T BELIEVE IT!

On average, the air breathed in and out through the night by a sleeping person, would fill an average-sized bedroom. This is why some people like to sleep with the door or window open!

349 There are more than 200 million tiny air bubbles, or alveoli, in each lung. Inside, oxygen from breathed-in air passes through the very thin linings of the alveoli to equally tiny blood vessels on the other side. The blood carries the oxygen away, around the body. At the same time a waste substance, carbon dioxide, seeps through the blood vessel, into the alveoli. As you breathe out, the lungs blow out the carbon dioxide.

Air in

Air out

Diaphragm
pulls down

Diaphragm
relaxes

▲ Breathing uses two main
sets of muscles, the diaphragm
and those between the ribs.

350 Breathing needs

muscle power! The main breathing
muscle is the dome-shaped
diaphragm at the base of the
chest. To breathe in, it becomes
flatter, making the lungs
bigger, so they suck in air
down the windpipe. At the
same time, rib muscles lift
the ribs, also making the
lungs bigger. To breathe
out, the diaphragm and
rib muscles relax. The
stretched lungs spring
back to their smaller size
and blow out stale air.

▶ After great activity,
the body breathes faster
and deeper, to replace
the oxygen used by the
muscles for energy.

Bronchiole

Blood
vessel

Air space
in alveoli

Alveoli

▲ Inside each lung, the main
bronchus divides again and again,
into thousands of narrower
airways called bronchioles.

351 As you rest or sleep, each breath

sends about half a litre of air in and out,
15 to 20 times each minute. After great activity,
such as running a race, you need more oxygen. So
you take deeper breaths faster – 3 litres or more of
air, 50 times or more each minute.

The hungry body

352 All machines need fuel to make them go, and the body is like a living machine whose fuel is food. Food gives us energy for our body processes inside, and for breathing, moving, talking and every other action we make. Food also provides raw materials that the body uses to grow, maintain itself and repair daily wear-and-tear.

353 We would not put the wrong fuel into a car engine, so we should not put unsuitable foods into the body. A healthy diet needs a wide variety of foods, which have lots of vital nutrients. Too much of one single food may be unhealthy, especially if that food is very fatty or greasy. Too much of all foods is also unhealthy, making the body overweight and increasing the risk of illnesses.

▶ It is important for children to learn how to cook healthily. Grilling or barbecuing food is much healthier than frying it.

▲ Fresh fruits such as bananas, and vegetables such as carrots, have lots of vitamins, minerals and fibre, and are good for the body in lots of ways.

▼ Foods such as bread, pasta and rice contain lots of starch, which is a useful energy source.

354 There are six main kinds of nutrients in foods, and the body needs balanced amounts of all of them.

- Proteins are needed for growth and repair, and for strong muscles and other parts.
- Carbohydrates, such as sugars and starches, give plenty of energy.
- Some fats are important for general health and energy.
- Vitamins help the body to fight germs and disease.
- Minerals are needed for strong bones and teeth and also healthy blood.
- Fibre is important for good digestion and to prevent certain bowel disorders.

◄ Fish, low-fat meats such as chicken, and dairy produce such as cheese all contain plenty of valuable proteins.

▲ Fats and oily foods are needed in moderate amounts. Plant oils are healthier than fats and oils from animal sources.

QUIZ

Which of these meals do you think is healthier?

Meal A
Burger, sausage and lots of chips, followed by ice cream with cream and chocolate.

Meal B
Chicken, tomato and a few chips, followed by fresh fruit salad with apple, banana, pear and melon.

Answer:
Meal B

157

Bite, chew, gulp

355 The hardest parts of your whole body are the ones that make holes in your food – teeth. They have a covering of whitish or yellowish enamel, which is stronger than most kinds of rocks! Teeth need to last a lifetime of biting, nibbling, gnashing, munching and chewing. They are your own food processors.

356 There are four main shapes of teeth. The front ones are incisors, and each has a straight, sharp edge, like a spade or chisel, to cut through food. Next are canines, which are taller and more pointed, used mainly for tearing and pulling. Behind them are premolars and molars, which are lower and flatter with small bumps, for crushing and grinding.

357 A tooth may look almost dead, but it is very much alive. Under the enamel is slightly softer dentine. In the middle of the tooth is the dental pulp. This has blood vessels to nourish the whole tooth, and nerves that feel pressure, heat, cold and pain. The lower part of the tooth, strongly fixed in the jaw bone, is the root. The enamel-covered part above the gum is the crown.

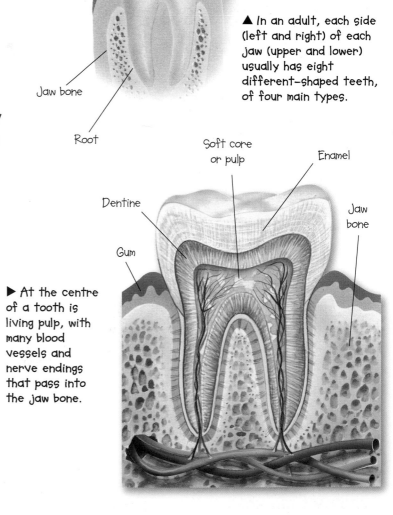

Incisor

Canine

Premolar

Molar

Jaw bone

Root

▲ In an adult, each side (left and right) of each jaw (upper and lower) usually has eight different-shaped teeth, of four main types.

Soft core or pulp

Enamel

Dentine

Jaw bone

Gum

► At the centre of a tooth is living pulp, with many blood vessels and nerve endings that pass into the jaw bone.

358
Teeth are very strong and tough, but they do need to be cleaned properly and regularly. Germs called bacteria live on old bits of food in the mouth. They make waste products which are acid and eat into the enamel and dentine, causing holes called cavities. Which do you prefer – cleaning your teeth after main meals and before bedtime, or the agony of toothache?

► Clean your teeth by brushing in different directions and then flossing between them. They will look better and stay healthier for longer.

▼ The first set of teeth lasts about ten years, while the second set can last ten times longer.

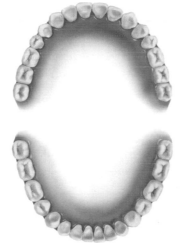

First set
(milk or deciduous teeth)

Second set
(adult or permanent set)

359
Teeth are designed to last a lifetime. Well, not quite, because the body has two sets. There are 20 small teeth in the first or baby set. The first ones usually appear above the gum by about six months of age, the last ones at three years old. As you and your mouth grow, the baby teeth fall out from about seven years old. They are replaced by 32 larger teeth in the adult set.

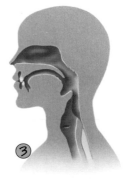

360
After chewing, food is swallowed into the gullet (oesophagus). This pushes the food powerfully down through the chest, past the heart and lungs, into the stomach.

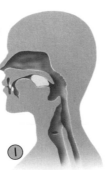
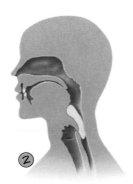

① Tongue pushes food to the back of the throat

② Throat muscles squeeze the food downwards

③ The oesophagus pushes food to the stomach

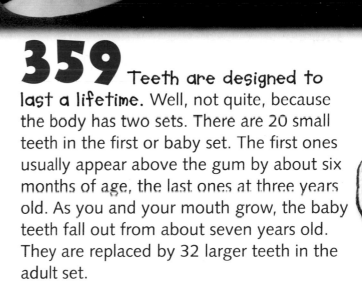

Food's long journey

361 The digestive system is like a tunnel about 9 metres long, through the body. It includes parts of the body that bite food, chew it, swallow it, churn it up and break it down with natural juices and acids, take in its goodness, and then get rid of the leftovers.

362 The stomach is a bag with strong, muscular walls. It stretches as it fills with food and drink, and its lining makes powerful digestive acids and juices called enzymes, to attack the food. The muscles in its walls squirm and squeeze to mix the food and juices.

363 The stomach digests food for a few hours into a thick mush, which oozes into the small intestine. This is only 4 centimetres wide, but more than 5 metres long. It takes nutrients and useful substances through its lining, into the body.

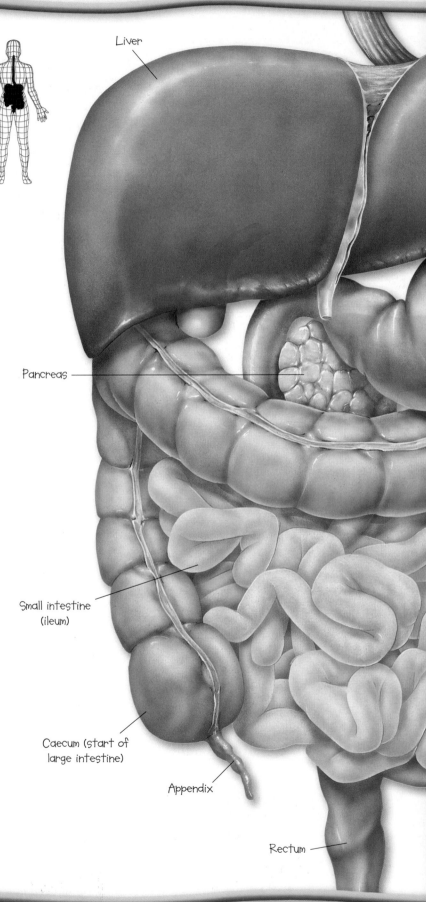

Liver

Pancreas

Small intestine (ileum)

Caecum (start of large intestine)

Appendix

Rectum

364

The large intestine follows the small one, and it is certainly wider, at about 6 centimetres, but much shorter, only 1.5 metres. It takes in fluids and a few more nutrients from the food, and then squashes what's left into brown lumps, ready to leave the body.

Stomach

Large intestine

Villus

Vessels inside villus

Vessels in intestine lining

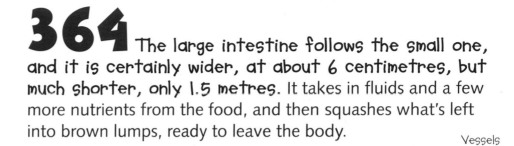

▶ The lining of the small intestine has thousands of tiny finger-like parts called the villi, which take nutrients from food, into the blood and lymph system.

◀ The digestive parts almost fill the lower part of the main body, called the abdomen.

365

The liver and pancreas are also parts of the digestive system. The liver sorts out and changes the many nutrients from digestion, and stores some of them. The pancreas makes powerful digestive juices that pass to the small intestine to work on the food there.

I DON'T BELIEVE IT!

What's in the leftovers? The brown lumps called bowel motions or faeces are only about one-half undigested or leftover food. Some of the rest is rubbed-off parts of the stomach and intestine lining. The rest is millions of 'friendly' but dead microbes (bacteria) from the intestine. They help to digest our food for us, and in return we give them a warm, food-filled place to live.

Blood in the body

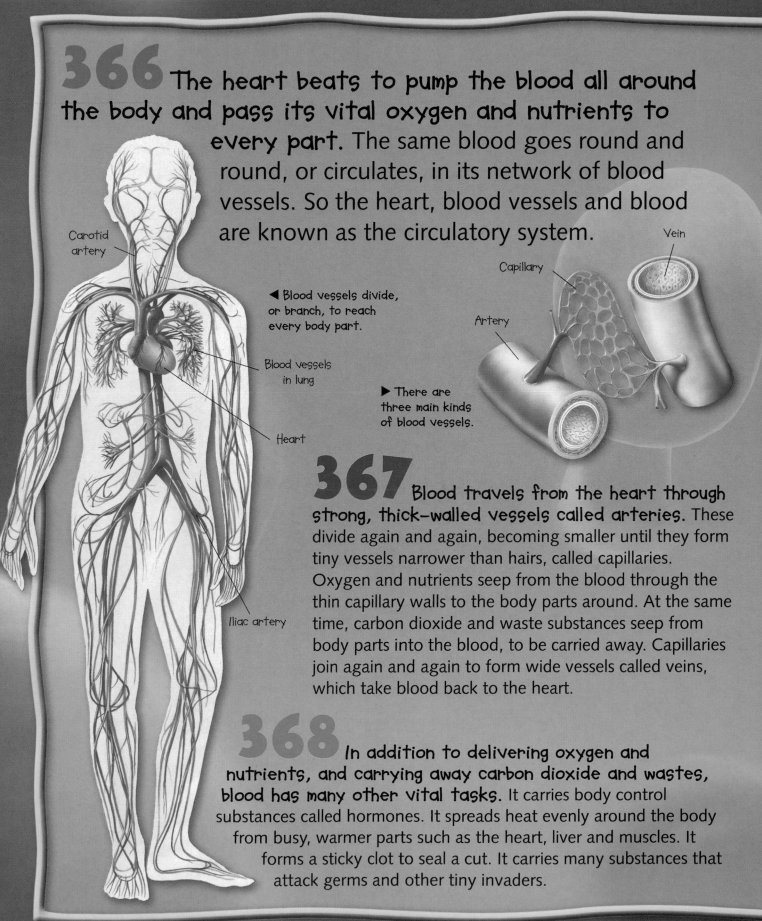

366 The heart beats to pump the blood all around the body and pass its vital oxygen and nutrients to every part. The same blood goes round and round, or circulates, in its network of blood vessels. So the heart, blood vessels and blood are known as the circulatory system.

Carotid artery

◀ Blood vessels divide, or branch, to reach every body part.

Blood vessels in lung

Heart

▶ There are three main kinds of blood vessels.

Iliac artery

Capillary

Artery

Vein

367 Blood travels from the heart through strong, thick-walled vessels called arteries. These divide again and again, becoming smaller until they form tiny vessels narrower than hairs, called capillaries. Oxygen and nutrients seep from the blood through the thin capillary walls to the body parts around. At the same time, carbon dioxide and waste substances seep from body parts into the blood, to be carried away. Capillaries join again and again to form wide vessels called veins, which take blood back to the heart.

368 In addition to delivering oxygen and nutrients, and carrying away carbon dioxide and wastes, blood has many other vital tasks. It carries body control substances called hormones. It spreads heat evenly around the body from busy, warmer parts such as the heart, liver and muscles. It forms a sticky clot to seal a cut. It carries many substances that attack germs and other tiny invaders.

369

Blood has four main parts. The largest is billions of tiny, saucer-shaped red cells, which make up almost half of the total volume of blood and carry oxygen. Second is the white cells, which clean the blood, prevent disease and fight germs. The third part is billions of tiny platelets, which help blood to clot. Fourth is watery plasma, in which the other parts float.

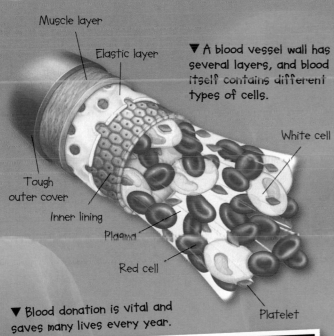

Muscle layer
Elastic layer
Tough outer cover
Inner lining
Plasma
Red cell
White cell
Platelet

▼ A blood vessel wall has several layers, and blood itself contains different types of cells.

▶ Each kidney has about one million tiny filters, called nephrons, in its outer layer, or cortex.

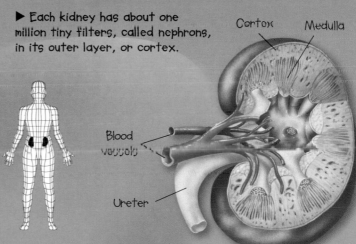

Cortex
Medulla
Blood vessels
Ureter

▼ Blood donation is vital and saves many lives every year.

AS-1 RED BLOOD CELLS
A Positive

370

Blood is cleaned by two kidneys, situated in the middle of your back. They filter the blood and make a liquid called urine, which contains unwanted and waste substances, plus excess or 'spare' water. The urine trickles from each kidney down a tube, the ureter, into a stretchy bag, the bladder. It's stored here until you can get rid of it – at your convenience.

The beating body

371 **The heart is about as big as its owner's clenched fist.** It is a hollow bag of very strong muscle, called cardiac muscle or myocardium. This muscle never tires. It contracts once every second or more often, all through life. The contraction, or heartbeat, squeezes blood inside the heart out into the arteries. As the heart relaxes it fills again with blood from the veins.

372 Inside, the heart is not just one bag-like pump, but two pumps side by side. The left pump sends blood all around the body, from head to toe, to deliver its oxygen (systemic circulation). The blood comes back to the right pump and is sent to the lungs, to collect more oxygen (pulmonary circulation). The blood returns to the left pump and starts the whole journey again.

▶ The heart is two pumps side by side, and each pump has two chambers, the upper atrium and the lower ventricle.

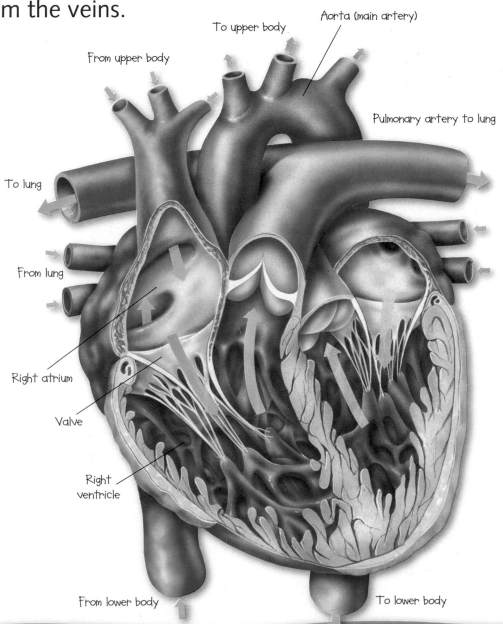

To upper body

Aorta (main artery)

From upper body

Pulmonary artery to lung

To lung

From lung

Right atrium

Valve

Right ventricle

From lower body

To lower body

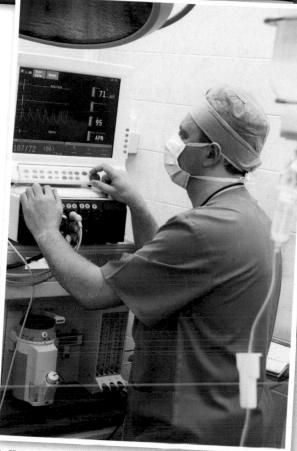

373
Inside the heart are four sets of bendy flaps called valves. These open to let blood flow the right way. If the blood tries to move the wrong way, it pushes the flaps together and the valve closes. Valves make sure the blood flows the correct way, rather than sloshing to and fro, in and out of the heart, with each beat.

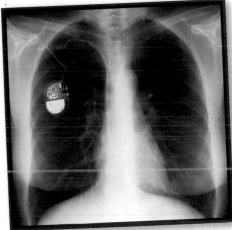

► This X-ray of a chest shows a pacemaker that has been implanted to control an irregular heartbeat.

▲ Doctors use ECG machines to monitor the electrical activity of the heart.

374
The heart is the body's most active part, and it needs plenty of energy brought by the blood. The blood flows through small vessels, which branch across its surface and down into its thick walls. These are called the coronary vessels.

375
The heart beats at different rates, depending on what the body is doing. When the muscles are active they need more energy and oxygen, brought by the blood. So the heart beats faster, 120 times each minute or more. At rest, the heart slows to 60 to 80 beats per minute.

HOW FAST IS YOUR HEARTBEAT?

You will need:
plastic funnel   tracing paper
plastic tube (like hosepipe)   sticky-tape

You can hear your heart and count its beats with a sound-funnel device called a stethoscope.

1. Stretch the tracing paper over the funnel's wide end and tape in place. Push a short length of tube over the funnel's narrow end.

2. Place the funnel's wide end over your heart, on your chest, just to the left, and put the tube end to your ear. Listen to and count your heartbeat.

Looking and listening

376 The body finds out about the world around it by its senses – and the main sense is eyesight. The eyes detect the brightness, colours and patterns of light rays, and change these into patterns of nerve signals that are sent to the brain. More than half of the information stored in the brain come into the body through the eyes.

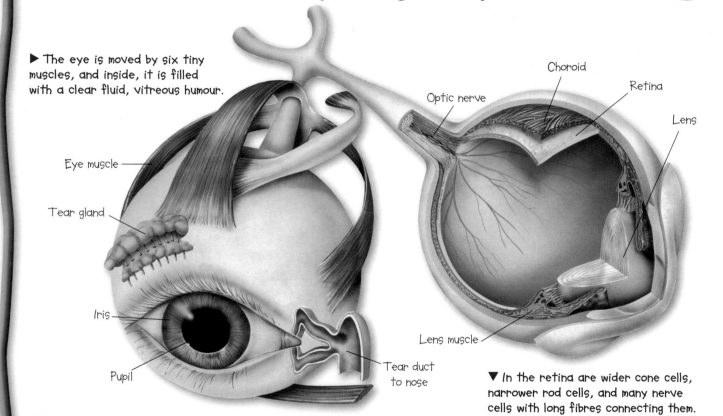

► The eye is moved by six tiny muscles, and inside, it is filled with a clear fluid, vitreous humour.

Eye muscle

Tear gland

Iris

Pupil

Tear duct to nose

Optic nerve

Choroid

Retina

Lens

Lens muscle

▼ In the retina are wider cone cells, narrower rod cells, and many nerve cells with long fibres connecting them.

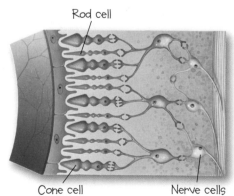

Rod cell

Cone cell

Nerve cells

377 Each eye is a ball about 2.5 centimetres across. At the front is a clear dome, the cornea, which lets light through a small, dark-looking hole just behind it, the pupil. The light then passes through a pea-shaped lens, which bends the rays so they shine a clear picture onto the inside back of the eye, the retina. This has 125 million tiny cells, rods and cones, which detect the light and make nerve signals to send along the optic nerve to the brain.

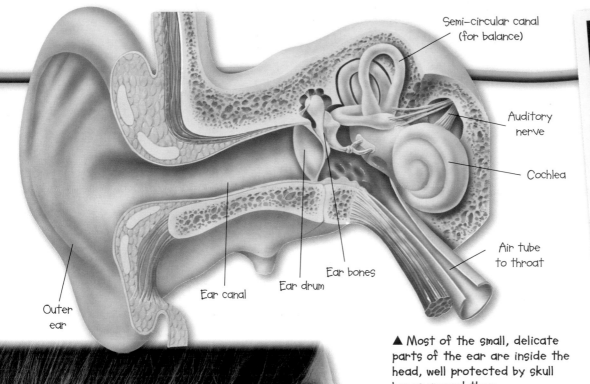

Semi-circular canal
(for balance)

Auditory
nerve

Cochlea

Air tube
to throat

Ear bones

Ear drum

Ear canal

Outer
ear

Atom bomb 210 dB

Jet take-off 140 dB

Thunder 100 dB

Talking 40 dB

Rustling leaves 10 dB

▲ Most of the small, delicate parts of the ear are inside the head, well protected by skull bones around them.

▶ The loudness, or volume, of sounds is measured in decibels (dB). Louder than about 90 dB can damage hearing.

◀ Some people need help to hear properly. A hearing aid worn inside the ear can help them to hear better.

BRIGHT AND DIM

Look at your eyes in a mirror. See how the dark hole which lets in light, the pupil, is quite small. The coloured part around the pupil, the iris, is a ring of muscle.

Close your eyes for a minute, then open them and look carefully. Does the pupil quickly get smaller?

While the eyes were closed, the iris made the pupil bigger, to try and let in more light, so you could try to see in the darkness. As you open your eyes, the iris makes the pupil smaller again, to prevent too much light from dazzling you.

378 The ear flap funnels sound waves along a short tunnel, the ear canal to the eardrum. As sound waves hit the eardrum it shakes or vibrates, and passes the vibrations to a row of three tiny bones. These are the ear ossicles, the smallest bones in the body. They also vibrate and pass on the vibrations to another part, the cochlea.

379 Inside the cochlea, the vibrations pass through fluid and shake rows of thousands of tiny hairs that grow from specialized hair cells. As the hairs vibrate, the hair cells make nerve signals, which flash along the auditory nerve to the brain.

Smelling and tasting

▼ The parts that carry out smelling are in the roof of the large chamber inside the nose.

Olfactory cells

Nasal cavity

Mucus lining

380 You cannot see smells, which are tiny particles floating in the air – but your nose can smell them. Your nose can detect more than 10,000 different scents, odours and fragrances. Smell is useful because it warns us if food is bad or rotten, and perhaps dangerous to eat. That's why we sniff a new or strange food item before trying it.

381 Smell particles drift with breathed-in air into the nose and through the nasal chamber behind it. At the top of the chamber are two patches of lining, each about the area of a thumbnail and with 5 million olfactory cells. The particles land on their sticky hairs, and if they fit into landing sites called receptors there, like a key into a lock, then nerve signals flash along the olfactory nerve to the brain.

▶ Olfactory (smell) cells have micro-hairs facing down into the nasal chamber, which detect smell particles landing on them.

Bone

Olfactory cell

Micro-hair

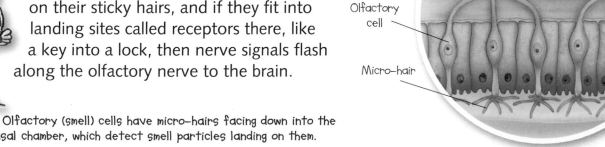

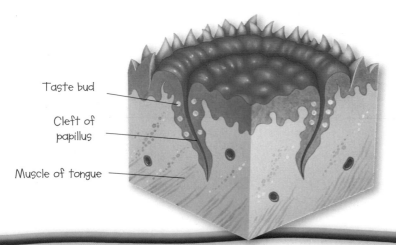

382 The body's most flexible muscle is also the one which is coated with 10,000 micro-sensors for taste — the tongue. Each micro-sensor is a taste bud shaped like a tiny onion. Most taste buds are along the tip, sides and rear upper surface of the tongue. They are scattered around the much larger flaps and lumps on the tongue, which are called papillae.

◄ The tongue is sensitive to flavours, texture and temperature.

383 Taste works in a similar way to smell, but it detects flavour particles in foods and drinks. The particles touch tiny hairs sticking up from hair cells in the taste buds. If the particles fit into receptors there, then the hair cell makes nerve signals, which go along the facial and other nerves to the brain.

Taste bud

Cleft of papillus

Muscle of tongue

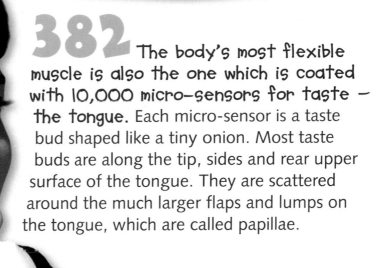

QUIZ

The tongue detects four basic flavours.

Which of these foods is sweet, salty, bitter or sour?

1. Coffee 2. Lemon 3. Bacon
4. Ice cream

Answers:
1. bitter 2. sour 3. salty 4. sweet

◄ The large pimple-like lumps at the back of the tongue, called papillae, have tiny taste buds in their deep clefts.

The nervous body

Brain

Spinal cord

384
The body is not quite a 'bag of nerves', but it does contain thousands of kilometres of these pale, shiny threads. Nerves carry tiny electrical pulses known as nerve signals or neural messages. They form a vast information-sending network that reaches every part, almost like the body's own Internet.

385
Each nerve is a bundle of much thinner parts called nerve fibres. Like wires in a telephone cable, these carry their own tiny electrical nerve signals. A typical nerve signal has a strength of 0.1 volts (around one-fifteenth as strong as a torch battery). The slowest nerve signals travel about half a metre each second, the fastest at more than 100 metres per second.

Sciatic nerve

Tibial nerve

Axon

◀ Nerves branch from the brain and spinal cord to every body part.

Dendrites

Synapse (junction between nerve cells)

386
All nerve signals are similar, but there are two main kinds, depending on where they are going. Sensory nerve signals travel from the sensory parts (eyes, ears, nose, tongue and skin) to the brain. Motor nerve signals travel from the brain out to the muscles, to make the body move about.

▶ The brain and nerves are made of billions of specialized cells, nerve cells or neurons. Each has many tiny branches, dendrites, to collect nerve messages, and a longer, thicker branch, the axon or fibre, to pass on the messages.

387

Hormones are part of the body's inner control system. A hormone is a chemical made by a gland. It travels in the blood and affects other body parts, for example, making them work faster or release more of their product.

388

The main hormonal gland, the pituitary, is also the smallest. Just under the brain, it has close links with the nervous system. It mainly controls other hormonal glands. One is the thyroid in the neck, which affects the body's growth and how fast its chemical processes work. The pancreas controls how the body uses energy by its hormone, insulin. The adrenal glands are involved in the body's balance of water, minerals and salts, and how we react to stress and fear.

▲ Sports such as snowboarding cause us to produce more adrenaline due to excitement and fear.

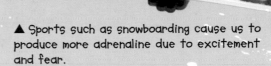

◀ Female and male bodies have much the same hormone-making glands, except for the reproductive parts — ovaries in the female (left) and testes in the male (right).

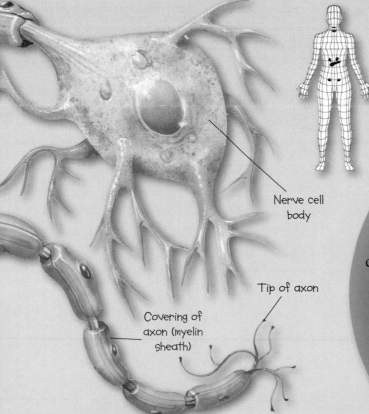

Nerve cell body

Tip of axon

Covering of axon (myelin sheath)

TIME TO REACT!

You will need:
friend   ruler

1. Ask a friend to hold a ruler by the highest measurement so it hangs down. Put your thumb and fingers level with the other end, ready to grab.

2. When your friend lets go grasp it and measure where your thumb is on the ruler. Swap places so your friend has a go.

3. The person who grabs the ruler nearest its lower end has the fastest reactions. To grab the ruler, nerve signals travel from the eye, to the brain, and back to the muscles in the arm and hand.

The brainy body

389 Your brain is as big as your two fists side by side. It's the place where you think, learn, work out problems, remember, feel happy and sad, wonder, worry, have ideas, sleep and dream.

▶ The two wrinkled hemispheres (halves) of the cerebrum, where thinking happens, are the largest brain parts.

390 The brain looks like a wrinkly lump of grey-pink jelly! On average, it weighs about 1.4 kilograms. It doesn't move, but its amazing nerve activity uses up one-fifth of all the energy needed by the body.

▼ Different areas or centres of the brain's outer layer, the cerebral cortex, deal with messages from and to certain parts of the body.

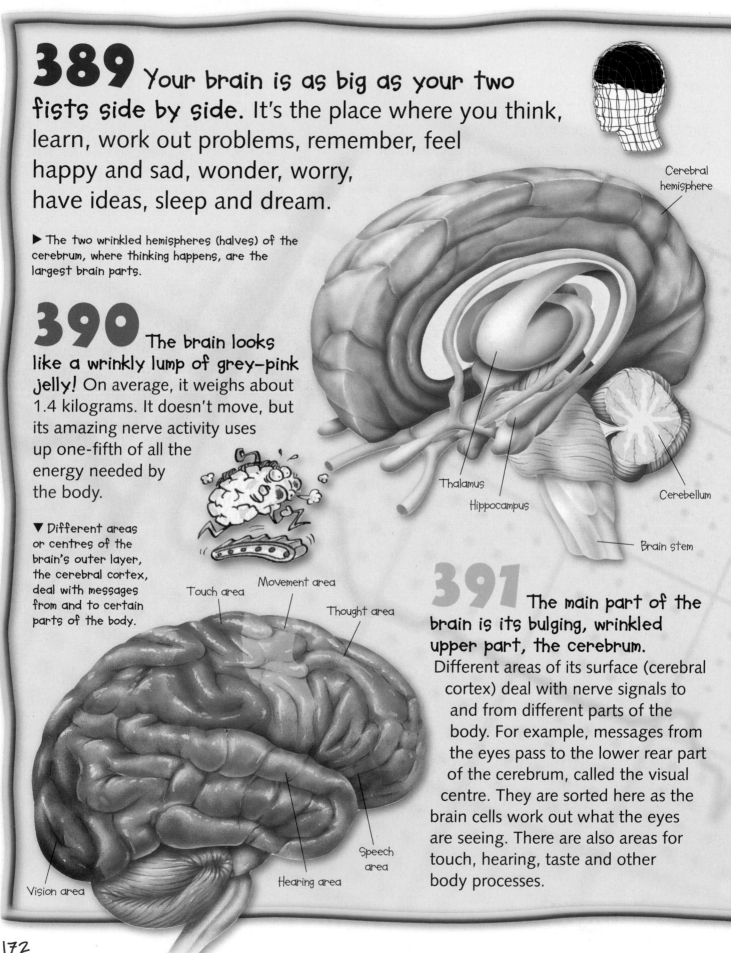

Cerebral hemisphere

Thalamus

Hippocampus

Cerebellum

Brain stem

Touch area

Movement area

Thought area

Vision area

Hearing area

Speech area

391 The main part of the brain is its bulging, wrinkled upper part, the cerebrum. Different areas of its surface (cerebral cortex) deal with nerve signals to and from different parts of the body. For example, messages from the eyes pass to the lower rear part of the cerebrum, called the visual centre. They are sorted here as the brain cells work out what the eyes are seeing. There are also areas for touch, hearing, taste and other body processes.

392 The cerebellum is the rounded, wrinkled part at the back of the brain. It processes messages from the motor centre, sorting and coordinating them in great detail, to send to the body's hundreds of muscles. This is how we learn skilled, precise movements such as writing, skateboarding or playing music (or all three), almost without thinking.

393 The brain stem is the lower part of the brain, where it joins the body's main nerve, the spinal cord. The brain stem controls basic processes vital for life, like breathing, heartbeat, digesting food and removing wastes.

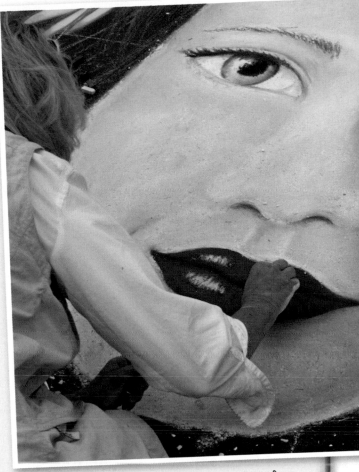

▲ Our brains allow us to draw from memory, expressing emotions.

394 The brain really does have 'brain waves'. Every second it receives, sorts and sends millions of nerve signals. Special pads attached to the head can detect these tiny electrical pulses. They are shown on a screen or paper strip as wavy lines called an EEG, electro-encephalogram.

▼ The brain's 'waves' or EEG recordings change, depending on whether the person is alert and thinking hard, resting, falling asleep or deeply asleep.

I DON'T BELIEVE IT!

The brain never sleeps! EEG waves show that it is almost as busy at night as when we are awake. It still controls heartbeat, breathing and digestion. It also sifts through the day's events and stores memories.

The healthy body

395 No one wants to be ill. Reducing the risk of becoming sick or developing disease is quite easy. The body needs a variety of different foods, especially fresh vegetables and fruits. And it needs the right amounts of these foods to avoid becoming unhealthily thin or fat.

396 Another excellent way to stay well is regular sport or exercise. Activity keeps the muscles powerful, the bones strong and the joints flexible. If it speeds up your breathing and heartbeat, it keeps your lungs and heart healthy too.

397 Germs are everywhere – in the air, on our bodies and on almost everything we touch. If we keep clean by showering or bathing, and especially if we wash our hands after using the toilet and before eating, then germs have less chance to attack us.

398 Health is not only in the body, it's in the mind. Too much worry and stress can cause many illnesses, such as headaches and digestive upsets. This is why it's so important to talk about troubles and share them with someone who can help.

▼ Germs on hands can get onto our food and then into our bodies. So it is important to wash hands before mealtimes.

399

Doctors and nurses help us to recover from sickness, and they also help prevent illness. Regular check-ups at the dentist, optician and health centre are vital. For most people immunizations (vaccinations) also help protect against diseases. It is good to report any health problem early, before they become too serious to treat.

▼ In some immunizations, dead versions of a germ are put into the body using a syringe, so the body can develop resistance to them without suffering from the disease they cause.

400

Old age is getting older! More people live to be 100 years or more and for many of them, their bodies are still working well. How would you like to spend your 100th birthday?

▼ Exercise keeps the body fit and healthy, and it should be fun too. It is always best to reduce risks of having an accident by wearing a cycle helmet for example.

INVENTIONS

401 **Humans have always been inventors.** More than one million years ago, our ancient relatives made simple stone tools. Around 30,000 years ago our more recent ancestors were much more skilled at tool-making (1) and they had worked out how to sew skins together to make clothes (2). The first musical instruments were made from bone more than 20,000 years ago (3). Early humans lived by hunting animals, and invented bows and arrows to which they added tips of sharp stone. Tools, clothes, weapons, dwellings and other inventions gradually became more complicated and numerous.

▶ Stone Age clothes were made out of animal skins sewn together using a bone needle.

The first inventions

402 The first inventors lived about 2.5 million years ago. They were small, human-like creatures who walked upright on two legs. Their first inventions were stone tools. They hammered stones with other stones to shape them. These rough tools have been found in Tanzania in Africa. Scientists call this early relative of ours 'handy man'.

Spear made from wood with tip of sharp flint

403 Stone Age people made really sharp weapons and tools by chipping a stone called flint. They dug pits and tunnels in chalky ground to find the valuable flint lumps. Their digging tools were made from reindeer antlers.

▲ Flint tools were shaped to fit comfortably into the hand, with finely chipped cutting edges that could cut through large bones.

404 Early hunters could kill the largest animals. They used flint-tipped weapons to overcome wild oxen and horses and even huge woolly mammoths. They used their sharp flint tools to carve up the bodies. The flint easily sliced through tough animal hides.

▼ Stone Age hunters trapped woolly mammoths in pits and killed them with spears and stones.

Stone

Pit covered with sticks

405

The axe was a powerful weapon. A new invention, the axe handle, made it possible to strike very hard blows. Fitted with a sharp stone head, the axe was useful for chopping down trees for firewood and building shelters.

▶ Axe heads were valuable, and were traded with people who had no flint.

MODERN AXE

▶ A modern axe is made of steel but it still has a long, sharp cutting edge and wooden handle.

▶ Saws were made from about 12,000 BC, and had flint 'teeth' held in place by resin.

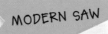

I DON'T BELIEVE IT!

Some Stone Age hunters used boomerangs! They made them out of mammoth tusks thousands of years before Australian boomerangs, and used them for hunting.

MODERN SAW

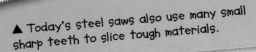

▲ Today's steel saws also use many small sharp teeth to slice tough materials.

406

Saws could cut through the hardest wood. Flint workers discovered how to make very small flint flakes. They fixed the flakes like teeth in a straight handle of wood or bone. If the teeth broke, they could add new ones. Saws were used to cut through tough bones as well as wood.

Making fire

407 People once used fire created by lightning. The first fire-makers probably lived in East Asia more than 400,000 years ago. As modern humans spread from Africa, over 60,000 years ago, they found that northern winters were very cold, and fire helped them stay warm. They discovered how to twirl a fire stick very fast – by placing the loop of a bowstring around the stick and moving the bow back and forth. After thousands of years, people invented a way to make sparks from steel by hitting it with a flint. Now they could carry their fire-making tinderboxes around with them.

▲ People discovered that very hot flames would harden, or 'fire', pottery in oven–like kilns.

▶ Fire provided early people with warmth, light and heat to cook food. The temperature deep within a cave stays the same whatever the weather outside.

MAKING HEAT

When your hands are cold you rub them together. Do this slowly. They feel the same. Now rub them together really fast. Feel how your hands get warmer. Rubbing things together is called friction. Friction causes heat.

408 Fire makes food taste good. Cooking food made it safer, as it kills germs, and cooking roots and meat makes them more tender and tasty. Humans are the only animals that cook food.

▲ Some people like cooking outdoors on a fire, as our relatives did over a quarter of a million years ago.

409 Humans invented lamps to light deep, dark caves. The lamps were saucers of clay or stone that burned animal fat, with moss for a wick. Campfire flames kept wild animals away at night. They also cooked food and kept people warm. People could see to make wall paintings in the caves.

New ways of moving

410 **With wheels you can move huge weights.** Once, heavy weights were dragged along the ground, sometimes on sledges – parts of 7000-year-old sledges have been found in Scandinavia. Then, more than 5500 years ago, the Sumerians of Mesopotamia began to make wheels from carved planks, which they fastened together.

Metal rim

Plank fastening

▲ Plank wheels were very heavy, and metal rims helped hold them together.

411 **Warriors had light, strong wheels on their fighting chariots.** Wheels with spokes are lighter than solid plank wheels. From about 1800 BC, the ancient Egyptians were using light chariots with spoked wheels. Horses pulled them fast in battle. The ancient Greeks and Romans used them for chariot races as well as for fighting.

Lightweight frame

Spoke

Light rim

◀ Spoked wheels made chariots light, fast and easy to steer.

1818

Hobby

1861

Velocipede (Boneshaker)

Early 1870s

Penny Farthing

1976   Mountain bike

412 Railway lines were once made of wood! Wheels move easily along rails. Horses pulled heavy wagons on these wagonways over 400 years ago. William Jessop invented specially shaped metal wheels to run along metal rails in 1789. Modern trains haul enormous loads at great speed along metal rails.

▲ The first public railway opened in 1825 and was 40 kilometres long. A century later, steam trains like this puffed across whole continents.

413 In 1861, bikes with solid tyres were called boneshakers! An even earlier version of the bicycle was sometimes called the 'hobby horse'. It had no pedals, so riders had to push their feet against the ground to make it move. The invention of air-filled rubber tyres made cycling more comfortable.

▲ Bicycle design has come a long way – early designs were very heavy, and had no pedals or way of steering.

QUIZ

Which came first?
1. (a) the chariot, or (b) the sledge?
2. (a) solid wheels, or (b) spoked wheels?
3. (a) rails, or (b) steam engines?

Answers:
1.b 2.a 3.a

▼ Wheels this size are usually only found on giant dump trucks. These carry heavy loads such as rocks or soil that can be tipped out.

414 Cars with gigantic wheels can drive over other cars! Big wheels give a smooth ride. At some motor shows, trucks with enormous wheels compete to drive over rows of cars. Tractors with huge wheels were invented to drive over very rough ground.

On the farm

415 The first farmers used digging sticks. In the area now called Iraq, about 9000 BC, farmers planted seeds of wheat and barley. They used knives made of flint flakes fixed in a handle made of bone or wood to cut the ripe grain stalks. The quern was invented to grind grain into flour between two stones.

▲ Curved knives made of bone or wood were used for harvesting grain.

▼ Ploughed furrows made it easier to sow, water and harvest crops.

416 Humans pulled the first ploughs. They were invented in Egypt and surrounding countries as early as 4000 BC. Ploughs broke the ground and turned over the soil faster and better than digging sticks. Later on, oxen and other animals pulled ploughs. The invention of metal ploughs made ploughing much easier.

I DON'T BELIEVE IT!
Some Stone Age people invented the first fridges! They buried spare food in pits dug in ground that was always frozen.

417 For thousands of years, farming hardly changed. Then from about 300 years ago a series of inventions made it much more efficient. One of these was a seed-drill, invented by Englishman Jethro Tull. Pulled by a horse, it sowed seeds at regular spaces in neat rows. It was less wasteful than the old method of throwing grain onto the ground.

Side seed-box

Main seed-box

Coulter bar

▲ Jethro Tull's seed-drill sowed three rows of seed at a time.

418 Modern machines harvest huge fields of wheat and other crops in record time. The combine harvester was invented to cut the crop and separate grain at the same time. Teams of combine harvesters roll across the plains of America, Russia, Australia and many other places, harvesting the wheat. What were once huge areas of land covered with natural grasses now provide grain for bread.

419 Scientists are changing the way plants grow. They have invented ways of creating crop plants with built-in protection from pests and diseases. Other bumper crop plants grow well in places where once they could not grow at all because of the soil or weather.

▼ The latest combine harvesters have air-conditioned, soundproofed cabs and nearly all have sound systems. Some even use satellite navigation (satnav or GPS receivers) to plot their route automatically around fields.

Under attack!

► One end of the spear thrower is cupped to hold the spear butt.

420 Using a spear thrower is like having an arm twice the normal length. They were probably invented over 20,000 years ago. Hunters and warriors used them to hurl spears harder and farther than ever before. People invented this useful tool all over the world, and Australian Aborigines still use it.

421 Arrows from a longbow could pass through iron armour. Bows and arrows were invented at least 20,000 years ago. More than 900 years ago, the English longbow was made from a yew branch. Archers used it to fire many arrows a long distance in a short time. By law, all Englishmen had to practise regularly with the longbow. It helped them win many famous battles.

► Bowmen often stood behind lines of sharpened stakes that protected them from enemies on horseback.

I DON'T BELIEVE IT!

Longbow archers could aim and fire six arrows per minute. The arrow sometimes went straight through an enemy's armour and out the other side.

422 Crossbows had to be wound up for each shot. They were invented over 2000 years ago in the Mediterranean area, and fired a metal bolt or short arrow. They were powerful and accurate, but much slower than longbows. Soldiers used them in sieges throughout Europe from about AD 1000 onwards. But in battles, where speed was important, crossbows were often beaten by longbows.

▶ Crossbows were the first mechanical hand weapons, and at one time the Church tried to ban them

423 In the Bible, David killed the giant, Goliath, with a pebble from a sling. The sling is an ancient weapon probably invented by shepherds. They used it when guarding their flocks, and still do in some countries. The slinger holds the two loose ends, and puts a pebble in the pouch. Then he whirls it round his head and lets go of one end. The pebble flies out at the target

▼ Modern catapults with extra-strong rubber fling stones 200 metres or more.

424 Even a small catapult can do a lot of damage. The rubber strips are like bowstrings, which can fire a pebble from a pouch, like a sling. Some anglers use a catapult to fire food to attract fish to the water's surface.

From stone to metal

425 Sometimes pieces of pure natural gold or copper can be found in the ground. The first people to work metal lived in the eastern Mediterranean around 8000 BC, and beat these metals with stone tools. They made the first copper weapons and gold ornaments.

▲ Gold is quite a soft metal. Early goldsmiths beat it into a variety of shapes and made patterns of hammered indentations on its surface to create beautiful objects.

426 Blowing air onto flames makes them hotter. About 8500 years ago people discovered how to melt metals out of the rocks, or ores, containing them. They invented bellows – animal-skin bags, to blow air onto the flames. The hot flames melted the metal out of the ore. We call this 'smelting' the metal.

▶ Bronze axe heads were sharper, and less easily damaged, than stone ones.

427 Bronze weapons stay sharper for longer than copper ones. About 5500 years ago, metal workers invented bronze by smelting copper ores and tin ores together. They used the bronze to make hard, sharp swords, spearheads and axe heads.

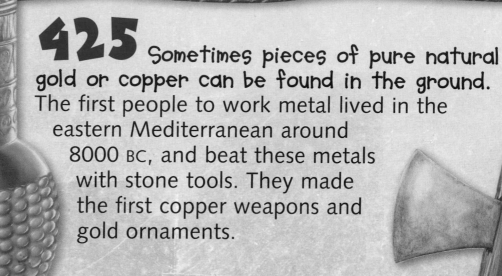

Bellows

Heat source

Molten bronze

Stone mould

◀ Molten bronze was poured into moulds of stone or clay to make tools.

▲ After smelting, iron was beaten into shape to make strong, sharp weapons.

▲ Iron chains arc made by hammering closed the red-hot links.

428 Armies with iron weapons can beat armies with bronze weapons. Iron is harder than bronze, but needs a very hot fire to smelt it. About 1500 BC, metal workers began to use charcoal in their fires. This burns much hotter than ordinary wood and is good for smelting iron.

429 The Romans were excellent plumbers. They made water pipes out of lead instead of wood or pottery. Lead is soft, easily shaped and is not damaged by water.

▼ At a smelting works metal ore is heated past its melting point and the liquid is poured to set in a mould.

430 Some modern steelworks are the size of towns. Steel is made from iron, and was first invented when small amounts of carbon were mixed into molten iron. Steel is very hard, and used to build many things, including ships and skyscrapers.

▶ Burj Khalifa in Dubai is the world's tallest building, at 829.8 metres. It has a steel framework weighing more than 4000 tonnes.

Boats and sails

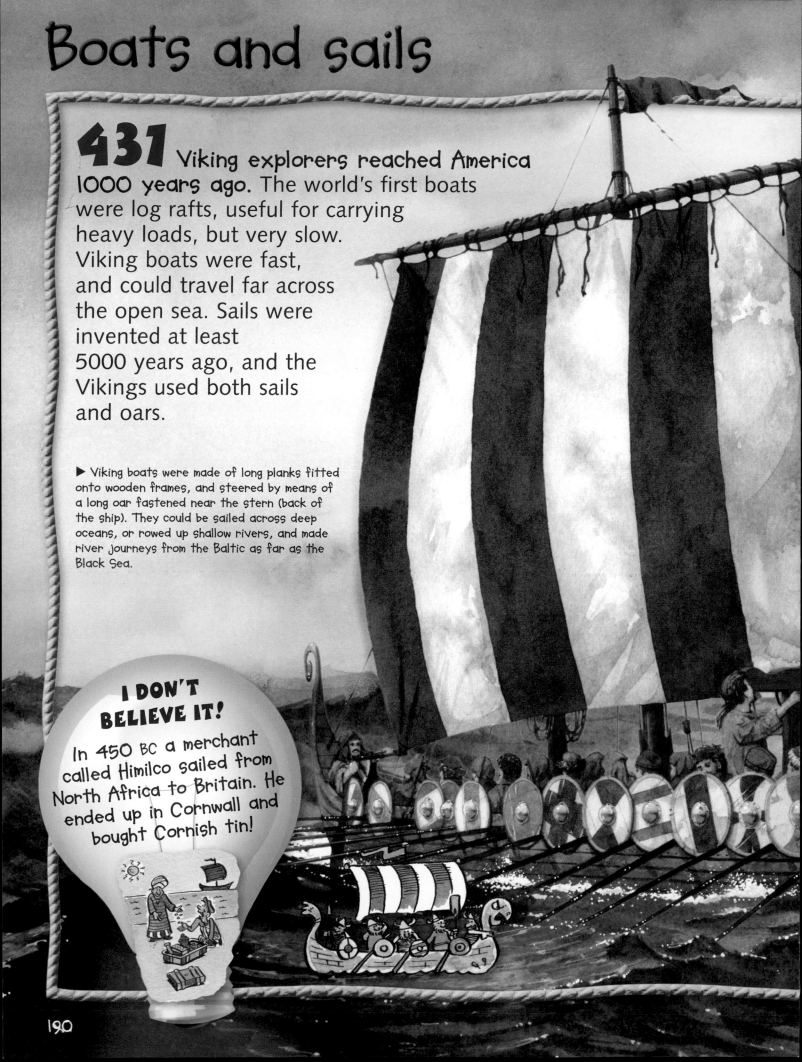

431 Viking explorers reached America 1000 years ago. The world's first boats were log rafts, useful for carrying heavy loads, but very slow. Viking boats were fast, and could travel far across the open sea. Sails were invented at least 5000 years ago, and the Vikings used both sails and oars.

▶ Viking boats were made of long planks fitted onto wooden frames, and steered by means of a long oar fastened near the stern (back of the ship). They could be sailed across deep oceans, or rowed up shallow rivers, and made river journeys from the Baltic as far as the Black Sea.

I DON'T BELIEVE IT!

In 450 BC a merchant called Himilco sailed from North Africa to Britain. He ended up in Cornwall and bought Cornish tin!

432 About 300 years ago sailing ships sailed all the world's oceans. Some, like the British man-of-war fighting ships, were enormous, with many sails and large crews of sailors. Countries such as Britain, France, Spain and Holland had large navies made up of these ships.

▲ Sailing ships called caravels, designed in the 1400s, were light, easily steered and ideal for exploring. Early ones had lanteen (triangular) sails, with square ones added later.

433 Some sailing boats race around the world non-stop. Modern sailing boats use many inventions, such as machines to roll up the sails and gears that allow the boat to steer itself. These boats are tough, light and very fast.

▶ Modern ocean-going yachts have a huge balloon-like sail called a spinnaker, invented in the mid-1800s. It is used mainly when heading in the direction the wind is blowing.

Wonderful clay

434 Stone Age hunters used baked clay to do magic. At least 30,000 years ago in Central Europe they discovered that some clay went hard in the sun, and even harder in a fire. They made clay figures of animals and humans, and used them in magic spells that they believed helped them catch food. Hardening clay in a fire was the start of the invention of pottery.

◀ By the year 500 AD in South America, Mayan craftsmen were 'firing' elaborate clay sculptures to make them hard and shiny.

▶ Kilns could produce much higher temperatures than open fires, and the heat could be controlled.

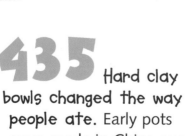

Clay pot

Heat duct

Fuel

MAKE A COILED POT

Roll modelling clay into a long, 'snake' shape. Coil some of it into a flat circle. Continue to coil, building the coils upward. Try and make a bowl shape, and finally smooth out the ridges.

435 Hard clay bowls changed the way people ate. Early pots were made in China over 15,000 years ago. They were shaped by hand and hardened in fires. They could hold liquid, and were used to boil meat and plants. This made the food tastier and more tender. Around 7000 BC, potters in Southeast Asia used a new invention – a special oven to harden and waterproof clay, called a kiln.

436 Potters' wheels were probably invented before cart wheels.

About 3500 BC in Mesopotamia (modern Iraq), potters invented a wheel on which to turn lumps of clay and shape round pots. By spinning the clay, the potter could make smooth, perfectly round shapes quickly.

437 Brick-making was invented in hot countries without many trees.

The first brick buildings were built in 9000 BC in Syria and Jordan. House builders made bricks from clay and straw, and dried them in the hot sun. By 3500 BC, bricks hardened in kilns were used in important buildings in Mesopotamia.

▲ As the clay turns around on the disc 'wheel', the potter applies gentle pressure to shape it into a bowl, vase, urn or similar rounded item.

438 Modern factories make thousands of pots at a time.

They are 'fired' in huge kilns. Wheels with electric motors are used, though much factory pottery is shaped in moulds. Teams of workers paint patterns.

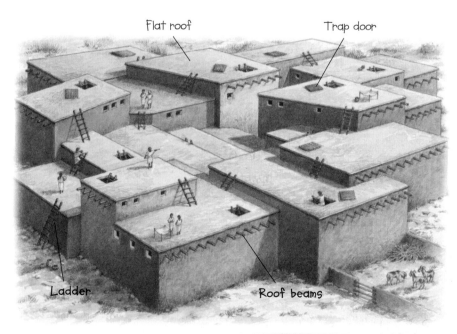

Flat roof Trap door

Ladder Roof beams

◀ With the invention of bricks, it was possible to construct large buildings. In 6000 BC, the Turkish town of Çatal Hüyük had houses with rooftop openings connected by ladders instead of doors.

Sailing into the unknown

439 Early sailors looked at the stars to find their way about. Around 1000 BC, Phoenician merchants from Syria were able to sail out of sight of land without getting lost. They knew in which direction certain stars lay. The north Pole Star, in the Little Bear constellation (star group), always appears in the north.

▲ Two stars in the Great Bear constellation are called the Pointers. They point to the north Pole Star in the Little Bear constellation.

440 Magnetic compasses always point north and south. They allow sailors to navigate (find their way) even when the stars are invisible. The Chinese invented the magnetic compass about 3000 years ago. It was first used in Europe about 1000 years ago.

◀ Compasses have a magnetized needle placed on a pivot so it can turn easily. Beneath this is a card with marked points to show direction.

441 Early maps showed where sea monsters lived. The first attempt at a world map was drawn by the Greek Ptolemy in AD 160. Greek maps of around 550 BC showed the known world surrounded by water in which monsters lived. Over 500 years ago, Pacific islanders had maps of sticks and shells, showing islands and currents. The first globe was invented in 1492 by a German, Martin Behaim.

▶ Using stick and shell maps, Pacific islanders successfully crossed thousands of kilometres of ocean.

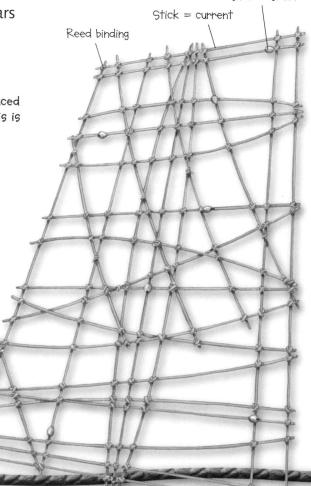

Shell = island
Stick = current
Reed binding

Mirrors

Telescope

Moving arm

▼ The chronometer was invented by Englishman John Harrison in 1735. It was a reliable timepiece, specially mounted to remove the effect of a ship's motion at sea.

▶ The sextant was developed around 1730 and was an important navigation aid until the 1900s.

Scale

442 Eighteenth-century sailors could work out exactly where they were on the oceans. They used an instrument called a sextant, invented around 1730. The sextant measured the height of the Sun from the horizon. The chronometer was an extremely reliable clock that wasn't affected by the motion of the sea.

USING A COMPASS

Take a compass outside and find out which direction is north. Put a cardboard arrow with 'N' on it on the ground pointing in the right direction. Then try to work out the directions of south, west and east.

▼ Modern navigation instruments use signals from several satellites to pinpoint their position.

Antenna (aerial) detects signals from available satellites

Batteries

Receiver compares the available satellite signals and 'locks on' to the three strongest ones

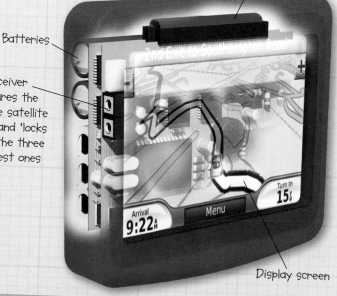

Display screen

443 New direction-finding inventions can tell anyone exactly where they are. A hand-held instrument, called a GPS receiver, receives signals from satellites in space. It shows your position to within a few metres. These receivers can be built into cars, ships, planes – even mobile phones!

Weapons of war

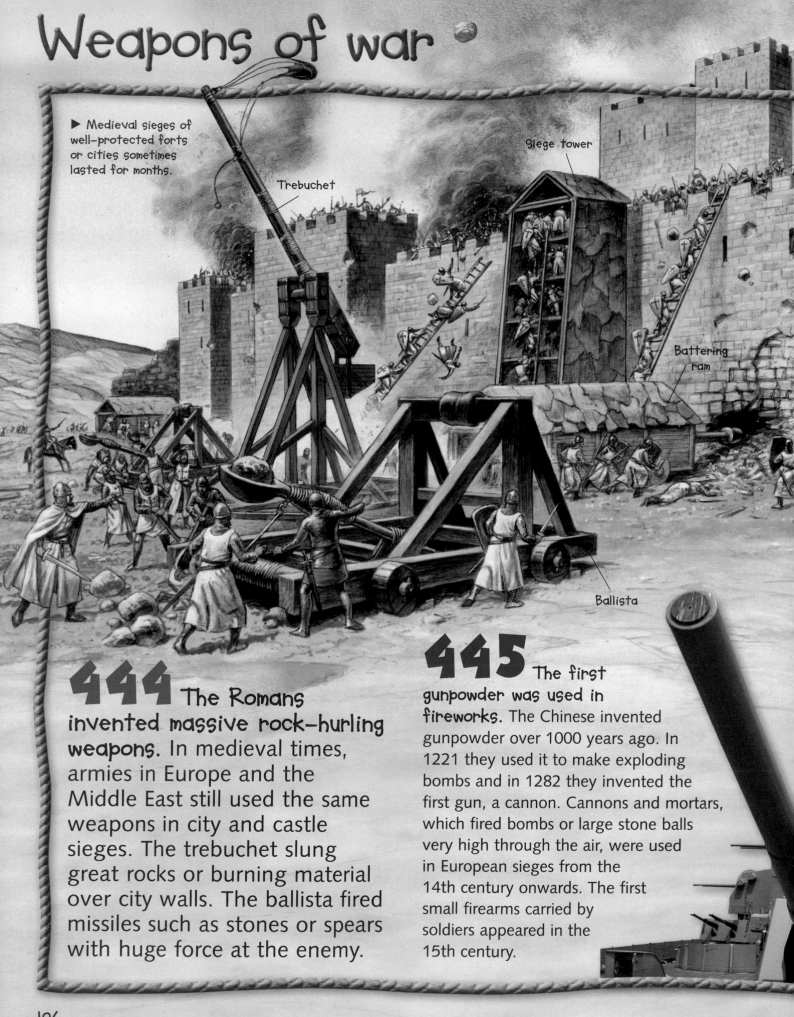

▶ Medieval sieges of well-protected forts or cities sometimes lasted for months.

Trebuchet

Siege tower

Battering ram

Ballista

444 The Romans invented massive rock-hurling weapons. In medieval times, armies in Europe and the Middle East still used the same weapons in city and castle sieges. The trebuchet slung great rocks or burning material over city walls. The ballista fired missiles such as stones or spears with huge force at the enemy.

445 The first gunpowder was used in fireworks. The Chinese invented gunpowder over 1000 years ago. In 1221 they used it to make exploding bombs and in 1282 they invented the first gun, a cannon. Cannons and mortars, which fired bombs or large stone balls very high through the air, were used in European sieges from the 14th century onwards. The first small firearms carried by soldiers appeared in the 15th century.

446

The battering ram could smash through massive city walls and gates. The Egyptians may have invented it in 2000 BC to destroy brick walls. It was a huge tree-trunk, often with an iron head, swung back and forth in a frame. Sometimes it had a roof to protect the soldiers from rocks and arrows from above.

I DON'T BELIEVE IT!

In 1453 the biggest cannon in the world could fire a half-tonne cannon ball one mile. It was used by the Turkish Sultan Mehmet to win the siege of Constantinople.

447

Gunpowder was used in tunnels to blow up castle walls. Attackers in a siege dug tunnels under the walls and supported them with wooden props. Then, they blew up or burned away the props so that the walls collapsed.

448

Greek fire was a secret weapon that burned on water. The Greeks invented it in the 7th century AD to destroy ships attacking Constantinople. A chemical mixture was squirted at enemies through copper pipes. It was still being used many centuries later in medieval sieges, pumped down onto the heads of attackers.

▼ The biggest battleship guns can hurl explosive shells more than 40 kilometres.

▲ The Gatling gun could fire six bullets a second.

449

Modern machine guns can fire thousands of bullets per minute. Richard Gatling, an American, invented a gun that would later lead to the development of the machine gun in 1862. As in all modern guns, each machine-gun bullet has its own metal case packed with deadly explosives.

Measuring time

450 The huge stone slabs of Stonehenge can be used as a calendar. Some of its stones are lined up with sunrise on the longest day of the year. It was built and rebuilt in Wiltshire in southern England between 3000 and 1550 BC.

▶ A sundial's shadow moves from west to east during the day.

Pointer

Hour markings

Shadow

▼ Raising the huge main stones of Stonehenge required the muscles of many workers and the know-how of skilled Bronze Age engineers.

451 One of the earliest clocks was a stick stuck in the ground. Invented in Egypt up to 4000 years ago, the length and position of the shadow gave the time of day. Later sundials had a face with hours, and a pointer that cast a shadow.

452

Candles, water and sand were all used to tell the time. The Egyptians used a clock that dripped water at a fixed rate from about 1400 BC. Candle clocks were marked with rings. In an hourglass (invented around AD 1300) sand ran between two glass globes.

▶ An hourglass shows a time period has passed, not the time of day.

◀ Until the invention of quartz movements, wristwatches contained springs and cogs.

Gear wheel

Ratchet wheel

453

You can't see any moving parts in a modern quartz clock. Early clocks depended on movement. A Dutchman, Christiaan Huygens, invented a clock in 1656 which depended on a swinging pendulum. About the same time, clocks driven by coiled springs were invented. Modern quartz crystal clocks work on invisible vibrations and are very accurate. They were first produced in 1929.

454

Some clocks are like toys. Swiss cuckoo clocks contain a bird on a spring that flies out of a little door and 'cuckoos' the time. Some 18th-century clocks looked like ships, and their guns fired to mark the hours.

▶ Wristwatches were not made until 1790. Many modern watches have a liquid crystal display (LCD) and show changing numerals instead of hour and minute hands.

MAKE A SHADOW CLOCK

Fix about 60 centimetres of garden cane upright in a flat piece of ground. Use lollipop sticks or twigs to mark the length and position of the shadow every hour, from 9 a.m. to 4 p.m., if possible. Which hour casts the shortest shadow?

Harvesting nature's energy

455 The first inventions to use wind power were sailing boats. Invented around 3500 BC by the Egyptians, and also by the Sumerians of Mesopotamia, the first sailing boats had a single square sail. By AD 600, windmills for grinding grain had been invented in Arab countries. Some European windmills, in use from about AD 1100 onwards, could be turned to face the wind.

456 The first waterwheels invented were flat, not upright. The ancient Greeks were using upright wheels more than 2100 years ago, and the Romans improved the design with bucket-like containers and gears to slow the turning rate. As well as grinding corn, some were used to drive pumps or saws.

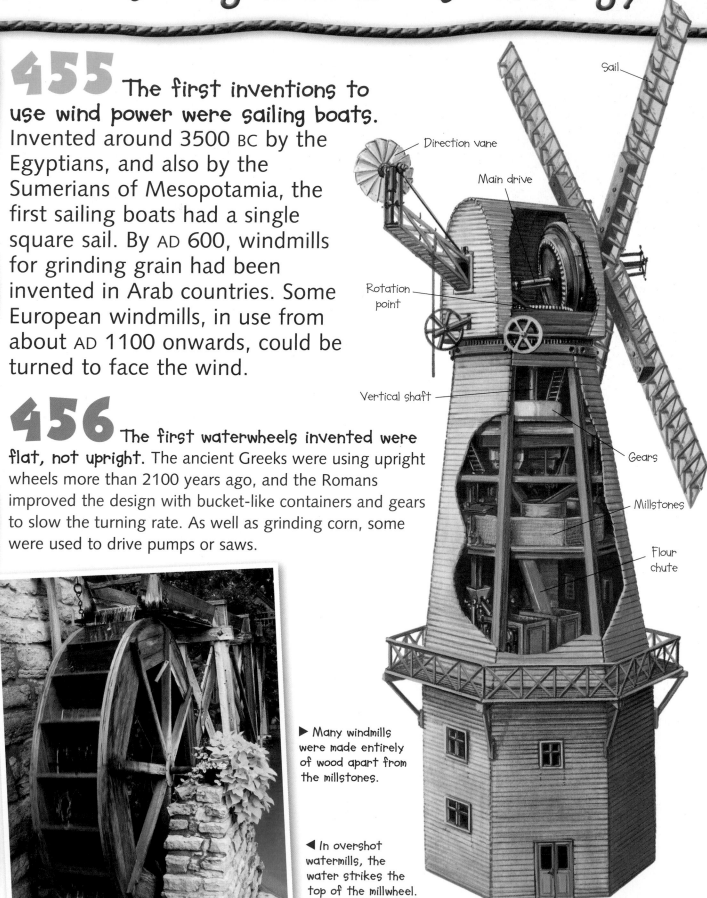

Sail

Direction vane

Main drive

Rotation point

Vertical shaft

Gears

Millstones

Flour chute

▶ Many windmills were made entirely of wood apart from the millstones.

◀ In overshot watermills, the water strikes the top of the millwheel.

200

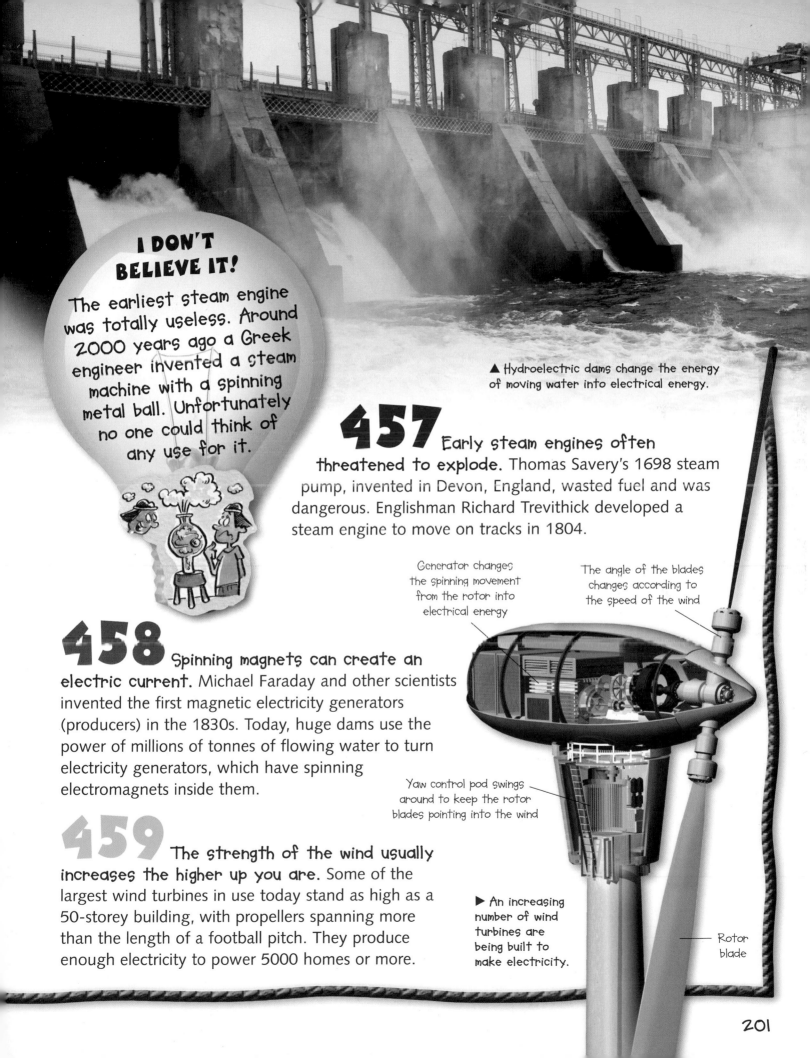

▲ Hydroelectric dams change the energy of moving water into electrical energy.

457 Early steam engines often threatened to explode. Thomas Savery's 1698 steam pump, invented in Devon, England, wasted fuel and was dangerous. Englishman Richard Trevithick developed a steam engine to move on tracks in 1804.

Generator changes the spinning movement from the rotor into electrical energy

The angle of the blades changes according to the speed of the wind

458 Spinning magnets can create an electric current. Michael Faraday and other scientists invented the first magnetic electricity generators (producers) in the 1830s. Today, huge dams use the power of millions of tonnes of flowing water to turn electricity generators, which have spinning electromagnets inside them.

Yaw control pod swings around to keep the rotor blades pointing into the wind

459 The strength of the wind usually increases the higher up you are. Some of the largest wind turbines in use today stand as high as a 50-storey building, with propellers spanning more than the length of a football pitch. They produce enough electricity to power 5000 homes or more.

► An increasing number of wind turbines are being built to make electricity.

Rotor blade

Marks on a page

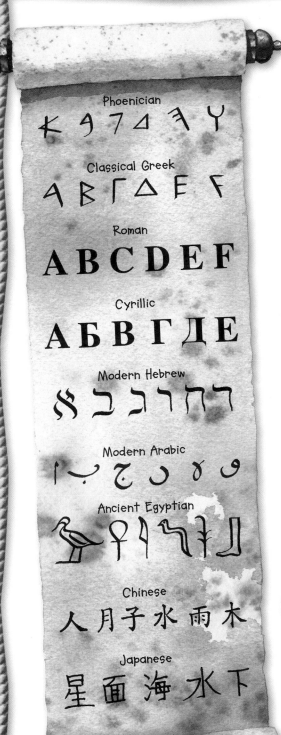

Phoenician

Classical Greek

Roman
ABCDEF

Cyrillic
АБВГДЕ

Modern Hebrew

Modern Arabic

Ancient Egyptian

Chinese
人月子水雨木

Japanese
星面海水下

▲ Ancient picture writing used hundreds of different signs, but most modern alphabets have far fewer letters.

460 **The first writing was made up of pictures.** Writing was invented by the Sumerians 5500 years ago. They scratched their writing onto clay tablets. The most famous word pictures are the 'hieroglyphs' of ancient Egyptians from about 5000 years ago. Cuneiform writing was made up of wedge shapes pressed into clay with a reed. It followed the Sumerian picture writing.

▲ Some of the religious books handwritten by monks were decorated with beautiful illustrations.

461 **The world's earliest books were rolls of paper made from reeds.** The first of this kind was produced in Egypt between 1500 BC and 1350 BC and was called 'The Book of the Dead'. Christian monks used to write their religious books on sheets of parchment made from animal skins.

462

Reading suddenly became much more popular after the invention of printing. A German, Johannes Gutenberg, was an early inventor of a printing press with movable letters in the 15th century. By the end of the century there were printing presses all over Europe.

◀▲ Early printing presses were made of wood, and used movable wooden letters.

463

Once, people were expert at doing sums on their fingers. The first written numbers were invented about 3100 BC by Middle Eastern traders. Around AD 300, the Chinese invented a counting machine called an abacus. It was a frame with beads strung on wires. Some people still use them.

Container of ink is punched open to release the ink, and pressurized to get the ink into the nozzle area

▼ Modern home printers build up the image as many tiny dots of ink forming a long row or line, and then another line next to it, and so on.

Print head zooms to and fro along a guide rail, squirting out tiny jets of ink

New sheets of paper are fed from the paper tray through a tiny gap by rubber rollers

Printed sheets pile up in the print tray

Power button

▲ Experts can do complicated sums very fast on an abacus.

464

Computers do sums at lightning speed. Early modern computers were invented in the United States and Europe in the 1930s and 1940s. Today, computers are small, cheap and extremely powerful. They can store whole libraries of information. The Internet allows everyone to share information and send messages immediately almost anywhere in the world.

I DON'T BELIEVE IT!

Some early Greek writing was called, 'the way an ox ploughs the ground'. It was written from right to left, then the next line went left to right, and so on, back and forth.

Making things bigger

▲ Spectacles became important as more people began to read books.

465 Small pieces of glass can make everything look bigger. Spectacle-makers in Italy in the 14th century made their own glass lenses to look through. These helped people to read small writing. Scientists later used these lenses to invent microscopes, to see very small things, and telescopes, to see things that are far away.

466 Scientists saw the tiny bacteria that cause illness for the first time with microscopes. The Dutch invented the first microscopes, which had one lens. In the 1590s Zacharias Janssen of Holland invented the first microscope with two lenses, which was much more powerful.

◄ Early microscopes with two or more lenses, like those of English inventor Robert Hooke (1635–1703), were powerful, but the image was unclear.

467 The Dutch tried to keep the first telescope a secret. Hans Lippershey invented it in 1608, but news soon got out. Galileo, an Italian scientist, built one in 1609. He used it to get a close look at the Moon and the planets.

QUIZ

1. Which came first, (a) the telescope, or (b) spectacles?
2. Do you study stars with (a) a microscope, or (b) a telescope?
3. Which are smaller, (a) bacteria, or (b) ants?

Answers:
1.b 2.b 3.a

468 Modern microscopes make things look thousands of times bigger. A German, Ernst Ruska, invented the first electron microscope in 1933. It made things look 12,000 times their actual size. The latest microscopes can magnify things millions of times.

◀ An electron microscope shows a tiny parasite in monstrous detail, but this tick is actually less than 15 millimetres long.

469 You cannot look through a radio telescope. An American, Grote Reber, invented the first one and built it in his backyard in 1937. Radio telescopes pick up radio signals from space with a dish-shaped receiver. The signals come from distant stars, and, more recently, from space probes.

▶ Most radio telescope dishes can be moved to face in any direction.

Making music

470 Humans are the only animals that play tunes on musical instruments. Stone Age people made rattles and similar noise-makers from mammoth bones and tusks. Instruments that you hit or rattle are known as percussion instruments, and are still used today.

▼ The instruments of the modern orchestra are grouped into sections according to type – usually string, woodwind, brass and percussion.

GUIDE TO THE ORCHESTRA

- **Percussion** instruments, such as drums, produce sound when they are made to vibrate by being hit, rubbed, shaken or scraped.

- **Brass** instruments, such as horns, are made of curled brass tubes. Sound is produced by blowing into a cup-shaped mouthpiece.

- **Woodwind** instruments produce sound when a player blows against an edge (as in flutes) or through a wooden reed (as in clarinets).

- **String** instruments have strings. They produce sound when their strings are plucked or bowed.

471 Over 20,000 years ago Stone Age Europeans invented whistles and flutes. They made them out of bones or antlers. Modern flutes still work in a similar way – the player covers and uncovers holes in a tube while blowing across it.

472 The earliest harps were made from tortoise shells. They were played in Sumeria and Egypt about 5000 years ago. Modern harps, like most ancient harps, have strings of different lengths.

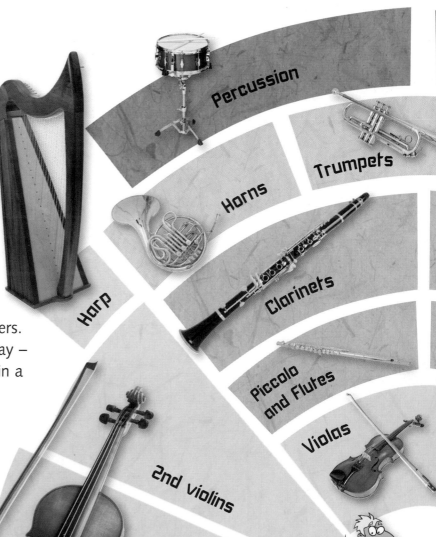

Percussion

Trumpets

Horns

Clarinets

Harp

Piccolo and Flutes

Violas

2nd violins

1st violins

Conductor

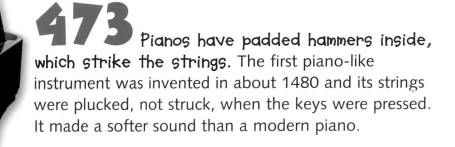

▲ The grand piano's strings are laid out horizontally in a harp-shaped frame.

Timpani

Trombones

Tubas

Bassoons

Oboes

Cellos

Double basses

473 **Pianos have padded hammers inside, which strike the strings.** The first piano-like instrument was invented in about 1480 and its strings were plucked, not struck, when the keys were pressed. It made a softer sound than a modern piano.

474 **The trumpet is among the loudest instruments in the orchestra.** A trumpet-like instrument was found in Tutankhamen's tomb in Egypt dating back to 1320 BC. Over 2000 years ago, Celtic warriors in northern Europe blew bronze trumpets shaped like mammoth tusks to frighten their enemies.

◄ The trumpet, played here by award-winning Alison Balsom, has a total tubing length of about 140 centimetres as well as three moveable valves.

475 **Bagpipes sound as strange as they look.** They were invented in India over 2000 years ago. The Roman army had bagpipe players. In the Middle Ages, European and Middle Eastern herdsmen sometimes played bagpipes while they looked after their animals.

► Some modern bagpipes still have a bag of sewn animal skins.

Keeping in touch

476 Some African tribes used to use 'talking drums' to send messages. Native Americans used smoke signals, visible several miles away. Before electrical inventions such as the telephone, sending long-distance messages had to be a simple process.

477 Wooden arms on tall poles across the country sent signals hundreds of miles in 18th–century France. Claude Chappe invented this system, now called semaphore, in 1797. Until recently, navies used semaphore flags to signal from ship to ship. In 1838 American Samuel Morse invented a code of short and long bursts of electric current or light, called dots and dashes. It could send messages along a wire, or could be flashed with a light.

◀ Skilled morse code operators could send 30 words per minute.

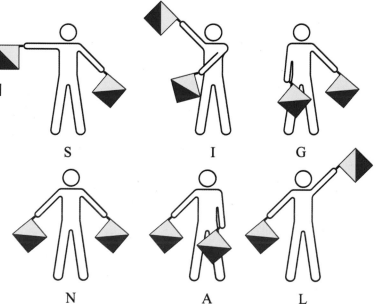

S   I   G

N   A   L

▲ Each position of the semaphore signaller's arms forms a different letter. What does this message say?

478 The telephone can send your voice around the world. A Scotsman, Alexander Graham Bell, invented it in the 1870s. When you speak, your voice is changed into electric signals that are sent along to a receiver held by the other user. Within 15 years there were 140,000 telephone owners in the United States.

Transmitter   Receiver

J.T.B. DEL.

▶ Bell's early telephone (top) in 1876 had one of the first electrical loudspeakers. The modern moving–coil design was invented in 1898 by Oliver Lodge.

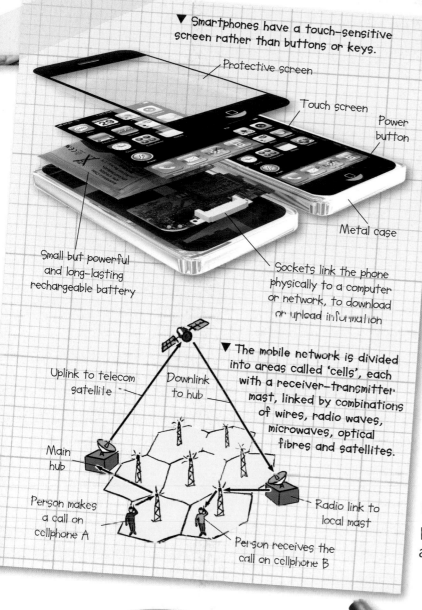

▼ Smartphones have a touch-sensitive screen rather than buttons or keys.

Protective screen

Touch screen

Power button

Metal case

Small but powerful and long-lasting rechargeable battery

Sockets link the phone physically to a computer or network, to download or upload information

Uplink to telecom satellite

Downlink to hub

▼ The mobile network is divided into areas called 'cells', each with a receiver-transmitter mast, linked by combinations of wires, radio waves, microwaves, optical fibres and satellites.

Main hub

Person makes a call on cellphone A

Radio link to local mast

Person receives the call on cellphone B

479

With a mobile or cellphone you can talk to practically anyone wherever you are. Your voice is carried on radio waves or microwaves and passed from antenna to antenna until it reaches the phone you are calling. Some of the antennas are on space satellites.

480

Radio signals fly through the air without wires. An Italian, Guglielmo Marconi, invented the radio or 'wireless' in 1899. Radio stations send signals, carried on invisible radio waves, which are received by an antenna. A Scot, John Logie Baird, invented an early TV system in 1926. TV pictures can travel through the air or along wires.

I DON'T BELIEVE IT!

Early TV performers had to wear thick, clownlike makeup. The pictures were so fuzzy that viewers could not make out their faces otherwise.

▶ Live TV images can be beamed to a satellite in space, then redirected to the other side of the world.

Taking to the skies

481 The first hot-air balloon passengers were a sheep, a duck and a cockerel. The French Montgolfier brothers invented the hot-air balloon in 1782. The first human passengers often had to put out fires, as the balloon was inflated by hot air created by burning straw and wool!

▲ The Montgolfier hot-air balloon made the first untethered, manned flight from Paris in 1783.

▶ The Wright Flyer had a spruce wood frame and canvas covering. It flew with the small wing at the front.

482 Many inventors have tried to fly by flapping birdlike wings. All have failed. One of the first bird-men crashed to his death at a Roman festival in the 1st century AD.

483 The first aircraft flight lasted just 12 seconds. The Wright brothers invented their airplane and flew it in 1903 in the United States. In 1909 a Frenchman, Louis Blériot, flew across the Channel. In World War I (1914–1918), planes were used in combat. In World War II (1939–1945), aircraft such as the British Spitfire beat off German air attacks.

► Da Vinci's helicopter used an 'air screw' popular in toys.

▼ Formed in 1965, the Royal Air Force Aerobatic Team, known as the Red Arrows, uses Hawk jets. They need perfect timing to perform their close formation flying and aerobatics at high speed.

484
Englishman Frank Whittle invented the first jet engine in 1930. Most modern aircraft are jets without propellers. Teams of jets, such as the Red Arrows, often perform stunts at air shows. In 1947 American Chuck Yeager flew faster than the speed of sound in the rocket plane Bell X–1.

485
The first model helicopter was made by Leonardo da Vinci as long ago as 1480. In 1877, an Italian, Enrico Forlanini, invented a model of a steam helicopter which flew for almost half a minute and reached a height of over 10 metres. Modern helicopters can hover and land almost anywhere, and are often used for rescue missions at land and sea.

I DON'T BELIEVE IT!

In 1783 the first hydrogen balloon was attacked and destroyed by terrified farm workers when it landed. It had flown 24 kilometres.

▲ The Westland Sea King, retired in Britain in 2011, was one of the world's most successful helicopters. It excelled at SAR (Search and Rescue), being able to hover steadily even in stormy winds.

Keeping a record

▼ Thomas Edison produced many important inventions, including sound recording, electric light bulbs and an early film-viewing machine.

486 **The first sound recording was the nursery rhyme, 'Mary had a little lamb'.** In 1877 an American, Thomas Edison, invented a way of recording sounds by using a needle to scratch marks on a cylinder or tube. Moving the needle over the marks again repeated the sounds. Performers spoke or sang into a horn, and the sounds were also played back through it.

487 **To play the first disc records, you had to keep turning a handle.** Emile Berliner, a German, invented disc recording in 1887. The discs were played with steel needles, and soon wore out. They also broke easily if you dropped them. Long-playing discs appeared in 1948. They had 20 minutes of sound on each side and were made of bendy plastic, which didn't break so easily.

▼ Early record players had to be wound up between records, and the loudspeaker was a large horn.

MODERN MUSIC PLAYER

▲ Digital music players can hold over two weeks of sound recording, played through earphones or a dock with speakers.

QUIZ

1. Were the first recordings on (a) discs, or (b) cylinders?
2. Which came first, (a) movies, or (b) long-playing records?
3. Was the first photograph of (a) flowers, or (b) rooftops?
4. The first movies were viewed through a hole in a box — true or false?

Answers:
1.b 2.a 3.b 4.True

488 It took eight hours to take the world's first photograph in 1826. Frenchman Joseph Nicéphore Niépce was the inventor, and the first photograph was of rooftops. Early cameras were huge, and the photos were on glass plates. In 1881 Peter Houston invented rolls of film, which George Eastman developed for the company Kodak, making photography much easier.

▲ Digital cameras have a display screen that shows the view the lens sees, which is the image that will be stored.

489 Only one person at a time could watch the first movies. The viewer peered through a hole in a box. Thomas Edison's company invented movies in 1888. The invention of a projector in 1895 by the French Lumière brothers allowed a whole audience to watch the film on a screen.

▲ The Lumière brothers, who invented the movie projector, also made films and opened the first public cinema.

► Launched in 2001, the iPod took little more than one year to develop.

490 The forerunner of the MP3 player was the portable laser-based CD player. It was more than ten times bigger and heavier than an iPod. Moving it often made the compact disc (CD) skip.

Round the house

491 **A horse and cart were needed to move the first successful vacuum cleaner around.** An English engineer, Hubert Cecil Booth, invented it in 1902. The first 'Hoover' electric vacuum cleaner was built from a wooden box, an electric fan and an old sack in 1907 in America.

▼ Refrigerators were once large, noisy and had little food space.

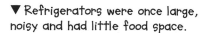

▲ Early vacuum cleaners worked by opening and closing a bellows with a handle.

492 Early refrigerators, invented in the 19th century, killed many people. They leaked the poisonous gas that was used to cool them. In 1929 the gas was changed to a non-poisonous one called freon. We now know that freon causes damage to the planet's atmosphere, so that has been changed too.

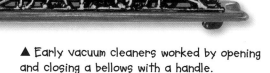

QUIZ

1. Did the first 'Hoover' need (a) a horse, or (b) an electric fan?

2. Were early refrigerators dangerous because (a) they blew up, or (b) they leaked poison gas?

3. The Cretans had china toilets 4000 years ago – true or false?

Answers:
1.b 2.b 3.False

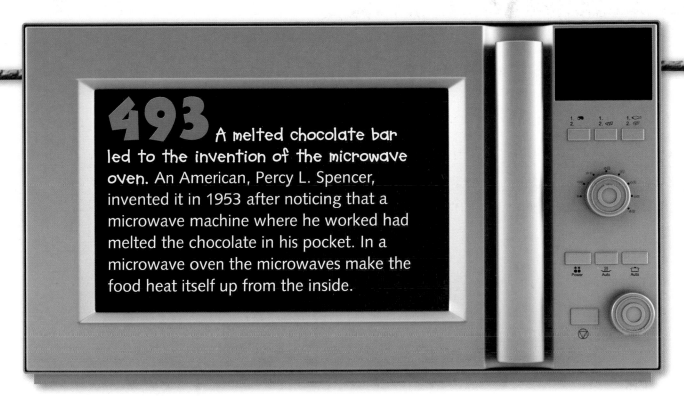

493 A melted chocolate bar led to the invention of the microwave oven. An American, Percy L. Spencer, invented it in 1953 after noticing that a microwave machine where he worked had melted the chocolate in his pocket. In a microwave oven the microwaves make the food heat itself up from the inside.

▲ In a microwave oven the microwaves are deflected by metal vanes down onto the food below.

494 There is no air inside a light bulb. If there was, it would burn out in no time. The first light bulbs failed because air could get in. American Thomas Edison invented an air-tight light bulb in 1879 that could burn for a long time. He opened the first electric light company in 1882.

▲ Energy-saving bulbs make light using fluorescence, where a chemical substance called phosphor lining the tube glows.

Vacuum bulb

◀ In a light bulb, electricity causes a wire filament to glow brightly in the airless bulb.

Filament

Screw thread

Power contact

495 Four thousand years ago in Crete in Greece the king's palaces had flushing toilets. They used rainwater. In England, toilets that flushed when you pulled a handle were invented in the 18th century. In 1885 Thomas Twyford invented the first all-china flushing toilet.

From Earth into space

496 Concorde flew at twice the speed of sound, nearly 2150 kilometres an hour. This is at least twice as fast as the earliest jets. The huge jet airliner crossed the Atlantic at a height of over 18,000 metres. All Concordes were retired in 2003.

497 Rockets helped the Chinese drive away a Mongol army in the 13th century.

The rockets used gunpowder, which the Chinese had invented 300 years earlier, but had only used in fireworks.

◀ The Chinese were the first to use gunpowder in war, as in this hand–held gun for firing missiles.

498 German war rockets in World War II (1939–1945) could travel 320 kilometres to hit England. They were invented by a scientist called Wernher von Braun. After the war he helped the United States build space rockets.

▼ German rocket pioneer von Braun designed the Saturn V rockets that launched the Apollo astronauts to the Moon. Here he shows an early version to US President Eisenhower.

I DON'T BELIEVE IT!

A 15th–century Chinaman, Wan Hu, tried to make a flying machine out of 47 rockets and two kites. His servants lit all the rockets at the same time, and Wan Hu disappeared forever in a massive explosion.

499 The Apollo II spacecraft landed the first men on the Moon in 1969. On Earth people watched on TV as Neil Armstrong and Buzz Aldrin stepped down onto the surface of the Moon.

500 The Space Shuttle travelled on a giant fuel tank with side rockets into space. Then the tank and rockets dropped away and the shuttle circled the Earth at a height of 241 kilometres. American scientists invented the reusable Space Shuttle, which first flew in 1981. The shuttles were retired in 2011.

◄ The Space Shuttle used rockets to enter space, but came back without them, landing on a runway like a giant glider.

Command module

Lunar module

Separation point

Separation point

3rd stage one J-2 engine

2nd stage containing fuel

Engines

Separation point

1st stage containing fuel

1st stage five J-2 engines

USA

▲ The three-stage Saturn V rocket carried the spacecraft of the first men to land on the Moon. It weighed over 2700 tonnes.

▼ The mighty Saturn V's forerunner was a tiny liquid-fuelled rocket, invented by Robert Goddard in 1926.

INDEX

Page numbers in **bold** refer to main entries; page numbers in *italics* refer to illustrations.

ACKNOWLEDGEMENTS

The publishers would like to thank the following sources for the use of their photographs:
t = top, b = bottom, l = left, r = right, c = centre, bg = background, m = main

Cover: Front(b) Power And Syred/Science Photo Library; Back(t–b) Kichigin/Shutterstock.com, York/Fotolia, Nikolay Petkov/Shuttertock.com, Racefotos2008/Shutterstock.com

Corbis 101 Robert Holmes; 128(l) Michele Eve Sandberg; 130–131 Jim Reed/Science Faction

Dreamstime.com 5(tl) and 20 Silverstore; 21(bg) Adam1975, 23(t) Paha_l; 36(tr) Zoom-zoom; 115(t) Wickedgood; 119(c), (b) Astrofireball; 133(b) Naluphoto; 137(b) Alangh; 138(b) Velkol; 153 Tobkatrina; 159 Kati1313; 171 Barsik

FLPA 103(b) Yva Momatiuk & John Eastcott/Minden Pictures

Fotolia 15(tl) Paul Heasman, (cr) Dariusz Kopestynski; 23(b) photlook; 36(third from tr); 147 chrisharvey; 149 Alexander Yakovlev; 167(r) Andres Rodriguez; 178–179(tc) Alexey Khromushin; 184(b) Rafa Irusta; 195(b); 203(cr); 205(t); 206(cl); 211(br) scazza; 216(tl) U.P. images; 217(tr) Sharpshot

iStockphoto.com 18–19(bg) Kevin Smith; 92(bl) David Mathies; 95(t) alohaspirit; 119(t) Scene_It; 120(m) Sean Randall; 133(t) luoman; 139(b) Rosemarie Gearhart; 188–189(bg) Sander Kamp; 197(br) Duncan Walker; 208(br) HultonArchive; 212(tl) hohos, (bl) James Steidl

NASA Images 2–3 and 73(cl) ESA, and the Hubble Heritage (STScI/AURA)-ESA/Hubble Collaboration; 52(tl), (bl), (bc); 53(cl) The Exploratorium; 57(tr), (br) JPL-Caltech; 58(tr) JPL/USGS, (b) JPL; 59(tr), (bl); 60 (br) Johns Hopkins University Applied Physics Laboratory/ Carnegie Institution of Washington; 62(c) JPL/University of Arizona, (bl), (br); 63(tr) JPL/Space Science Institute, (bl) E. Karkoschka (University of Arizona); 64(tl) ESA, and L. Lamy (Observatory of Paris, CNRS, CNES); 65(cl); 69(tr) ESA/STScI; 70(tr), (bl) ESA, K. Noll (STScI), (br) H. Richer (University of British Columbia); 71(tr) JPL-Caltech/STScI/CXC/SAO, (br) NASA/CXC; 73(tr), (tl) CXC/KIPAC/S.Allen et al; Radio: NRAO/VLA/G.Taylor; Infrared: NASA/ESA/McMaster Univ./W.Harris; (bl) ESA, A. Nota (ESA/STScI) et al, (br) ESA, M. Livio (STScI) and the Hubble Heritage Team (STScI/AURA); 74(bl) ESA, M. Postman (STScI), and the CLASH Team, (cr); 77(t); 79(l), (m) Dick Clark; 80(tr); 81(b); 83(tr); 85(tr); 88(t); 90(m), (l); 100(bl) NASA/JPL/UCSD/JSC; 130(t) NASA/Lori Losey; 131(tl) Jesse Allen, Earth Observatory; 216(br) NASA Marshall Space Flight Center (NASA-MSFC); 217(bl) NASA Stennis Space Center, (br) NASA MSFC

photolibrary.com 19(b) Laguna Design

Rex features 107(m) KeystoneUSA-ZUMA; 207(c)

Science Photo Library 61(m) Mark Garlick; 68–69(m) Mark Garlick; 102–103(m) Gary Hincks

Shutterstock.com 1 Sebastian Kaulitzki; 6(tl) and 112–113 kornilov007, (cl) Kichigin, (cr) Lightspring, (br) Milunkic; 8–9 ssguy; 7(tr) and 189(c) Oleg – F; 10–11 Sergey Lavrentev; 11(t) Ljupco Smokovski; 12(bg) Deymos, (tr) Vakhrushev Pavel, (b) Ivonne Wierink; 13(t) w shane dougherty; 14(tr) yuyangc; 16(m) yxm2008, (bl) ARENA Creative; 17(b) Tatiana Makotra; 22(bg) asharkyu, (cr) Eimantas Buzasl; 24–25(m) vadim kozlovsky; 26–27(bg) Gunnar Pippel; 26(b) Smileus; 27(c) Ray Hub; 28(c) Sebastian Crocker; 29(b) Hywit Dimyadi; 30–31(bg) archibald, (c) ifong; 31(tl) Viktor Gmyria; 32–33(bg) Redshinestudio; 33(all) Annette Shaff; 34 Jaggat; 35(c) michael rubin; 36(second from tr) Maksim Toome, (from fourth from tr) Balazs Toth, CaptureLight, Jaochainoi; 42(tl) Kurhan, (br) Tamara Kulikova; 43(t) Alexander Raths, (b) Kirsty Pargeter; 45(t) wim claes, (b) indiangypsy; 46(m) beerkoff, (bl) Smit; 49(tr) Morgan Lane Photography, (b) ssuaphotos; 53(bl) Dimec; 56(bl) tororo reaction; 66 MarcelClemens; 67(b) Action Sports Photography; 72(m) John A Davis; 76(tr/cl) Eky Studio, (br) Karin Wassmer; 77(m) Manamana; 90(cr) Elisei Shafer, (cr) Thomas Barrat, (br) javarman; 92(tl) Seriousjoy, (c) Kevin Eaves, (br) Asaf Eliason; 93(tl) haveseen, (tr) Wild Arctic Pictures, (c) Pichugin Dmitry, (br) Oleg Znamenskiy, (bl) Tatiana Popova; 94(t) Redsapphire; 96(m) 1000 Words, (tr) Morozova Oxana, (b) Mark Sayer; 97(b) Dmitriy Bryndin; 98–99(m) Roca; 99(t) Loskutnikov; 102(b) Alexandr Zyryanov; 105(b) Christy Nicholas; 106(t) Olivier Le Queinec, (b) Mike Buchheit; 108(m) Bull's-Eye Arts; 109(tl) Brandelet, (tr) Mikhail Pogosov, (b) Armin Rose; 110(t) @cam; 111(bl) Stephen Meese, (Force 0) Tudor Spinu, (Force 1) Sinelyov, (Force 2) Jennifer Griner, (Force 4) Vlue, (Force 5) Martin Preston, (Force 6) behindlens, (Force 7) photobank.kiev.ua, (Force 8) Robert Hoetink, (Force 9) Slobodan Djajic, (Force 10) Ortodox, (Force 11) Dustie, (Force 12) Melissa Brandes; 113(bl) Sam DCruz, (c) Gunnar Pippel, (tl) Jack Dagley Photography; 117(bl) DarkOne, (br) javarman; 118(m) PhotoHouse, (bl) pzAxe; 120(t) EcoPrint; 121(t) outdoorsman, (b) Jean-Edouard Rozey; 123(l) Patryk Kosmider, (r) riekephotos; 124(m) AdamEdwards; 125(t) photomaster; 125(b) Squarciomomo; 126(t) Khirman Vladimir, 126–127(b) Steve Mann; 127(c) AISPIX by Image Source; 129(b) Map Resources; 132(m) Lee Prince; 134(t) and 135(br) fotoluminate, 134–135 jan kranendonk; 139(t) Kozlovskaya Ksenia; 140 Lilya Espinosa; 141 Stanislav Fridkin; 142(blonde) Jeanne Hatch, (straight black) wong sze yuen, (curly black) Felix Mizioznikov; 143(l) Steven Chiang, (r) Carmen Steiner; 146 konmesa; 150–151 PiLart; 150 Taranova; 151 Jaren Jai Wicklund; 152 JonMilnes; 155 Lawrence Wee; 156–157 Elena Schweitzer; 156(bl) Yuri Arcurs; 159 Kati1313; 162–163(bg) Sebastian Kaulitzki; 165(tr) beerkoff; 167(l) Paul Matthew Photography; 169 Elena Elisseeva; 173 Sebastien Burel; 174 picturepartners; 175 Monkey Business Images; 178–179(bg) Mark Carrel; 179(cr) Richard Peterson, (br) Fedorov Oleksiy; 180(tr) Marijus Auruskevicius; 181(tr) Maksym Gorpenyuk; 183(tl) Bernd Juergens, (br) Michael Stokes; 185(b) Orientaly; 187(br) Julija Sapic; 189(r) Kjersti Joergensen; 191(br) Darren Baker; 192(tl) Irafael; 193(tr) Thirteen; 194(l) Alex Staroseltsev; 197(bl K. L. Kohn; 198(t) Awe Inspiring Images; 199(c) Galushko Sergey, (bc) Indigo Fish, (tr) Ispace; 200(bl) Geoffrey Kuchera; 201(t) Alexandru Chririac; 203(tl) marekuliasz, (bl) Lim Yong Hian; 204(tl) alexnika; 205(m) Caitlin Mirra; 206(violas) Milan Vasicek; (conductor) HitToon.com; 207(br) Stephen Meese; 208(l) EW CHEE GUAN, (cr) Barry Barnes, (b) Pakhnyushcha; 209(br) Alexandr Kolupayev; 210–211(m) Becky Stares; 211(tr) c.; 213(cl) Gordan, (bl) drfelice; 215(t) Maksym Bondarchuk, (bl) steamroller_blues, (br) Slaven; 216–217(bg) plavusa87

Wikimedia commons 99(c) Arthur Rothstein; 127(b) Olof Arenius

All other photographs are from: digitalSTOCK, digitalvision, Dreamstime.com, Fotolia.com, ImageState, iStockphoto.com, John Foxx, PhotoAlto, PhotoDisc, PhotoEssentials, PhotoPro, Stockbyte

All artworks from the Miles Kelly Artwork Bank

Every effort has been made to acknowledge the source and copyright holder of each picture. Miles Kelly Publishing apologizes for any unintentional errors or omissions.

224

Alec

Congratulations on your
First Holy Communion

with love from

Dominic, Dawn, Alex and Charlotte
xxxx